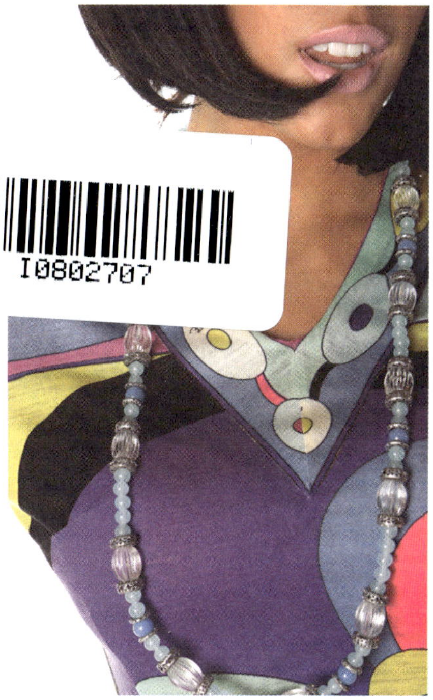

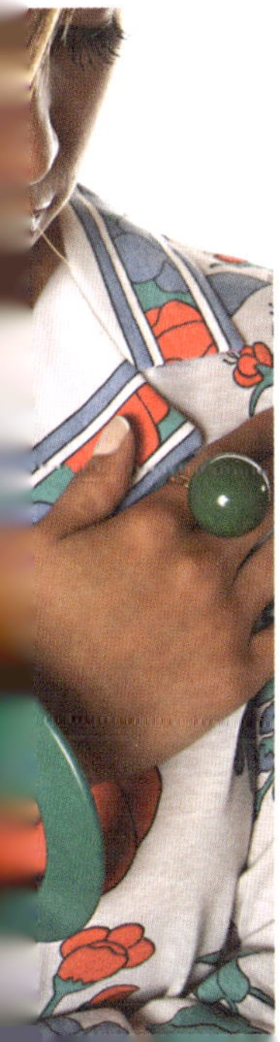

SIGNATURE PRINTS

Jet Set Glamour of the '60s & '70s

Written & Styled by

ROSEANN ETTINGER

Photography by Rich Cutrone

Schiffer Publishing Ltd

4880 Lower Valley Road Atglen, Pennsylvania 19310

Dedication

To Terry Ettinger,
my husband, best friend,
and the father of my four beautiful children.

Title page photo: The Pucci double-breasted jacket and silk jersey fringed dress compliment each other perfectly. The rhinestone jewelry and high-heeled sandals were added for a more glamorous look.

Captions for photos at right:
1. Notice the Aremis signature on the leaf.
2. Spring and fall Lilly Pulitzer fashions as advertised in *Vogue*, April and November of 1970.
3. Spring and summer Lilly Pulitzer fashions as advertised in *Harper's Bazaar,* March and June of 1971
4. Men's printed blazer and a woman's summer shift by Lilly Pulitzer as advertised in *Harper's Bazaar* in July of 1971.
5. "Pier 21" print made of Antron nylon and Lycra spandex designed by Gene Berk for Paganne as seen in *Harper's Bazaar* in December of 1973.
6. Vera knit tunic top and matching pants in brown, black and white with an abstract print. This outfit was offered for sale in November of 1970.

Library of Congress Control Number: 2007940872

Type set in Eras Md BT/Dutch 809 BT

ISBN: 978-0-7643-2896-1

Printed in China

Published by Schiffer Publishing Ltd.
4880 Lower Valley Road
Atglen, PA 19310
Phone: (610) 593-1777; Fax: (610) 593-2002
E-mail: Info@schifferbooks.com

For the largest selection of fine reference books on this and related subjects, please visit our web site at **www.schifferbooks.com**
We are always looking for people to write books on new and related subjects. If you have an idea for a book please contact us at the above address.

This book may be purchased from the publisher.
Include $3.95 for shipping.
Please try your bookstore first.
You may write for a free catalog.

In Europe, Schiffer books are distributed by
Bushwood Books
6 Marksbury Ave.
Kew Gardens
Surrey TW9 4JF England
Phone: 44 (0) 20 8392-8585; Fax: 44 (0) 20 8392-9876
E-mail: info@bushwoodbooks.co.uk
Website: www.bushwoodbooks.co.uk
Free postage in the U.K., Europe; air mail at cost.

CONTENTS

ACKNOWLEDGMENTS

Words cannot express my gratitude to my wonderful family for helping to make this book emerge from a dream that it would become reality. My husband, Terry, helped the photographer set up a studio and kept everything in order during the intense photography sessions. My daughter Amber Lee took time from her busy schedule to work on this project with professionalism, poise, and creativity in front of the camera. My son Clint assisted with the men's clothing, especially Pucci attire. My daughters Lexie, who helped type the manuscript, and Sabrina, who had a blast working with the great signature scarves, kept me focused. Without them all, this book would not have been possible. I graciously thank Rich Cutrone, my wonderful photographer, who listened while I explained the project and did exactly what I envisioned. His sensational photographs display the beauty of the prints. Peter and Nancy Schiffer gave me an opportunity to be totally creative with this project and never doubted my ideas. Thank you all so much!

PREFACE

Almost a decade ago, as I wrote the book *Psychedelic Chic,* I stumbled upon a treasure trove of sixties and seventies fashions that made a huge impact on me. The clothing's colors, prints, and fabrics were intoxicating. I couldn't stop looking at these garments and thinking about what it would have been like to wear them when they were first introduced, when I was just a teenager. I remember hearing the name Emilio Pucci and being referenced to expensive "psychedelic" prints, but that was all I could recall. As my research for *Psychedelic Chic* continued, I searched the internet for more Pucci dresses and began to see a trend: buyers were selling dresses that looked like Pucci designs and felt like Pucci fabric, but in fact were "Pucci-esque," "Pucci-style," and even called "pseudo-Pucci." Many of these dresses had signatures discreetly placed in their elaborate prints, but they didn't read "Emilio." Instead, names like *Mr. Dino, Paganne, Eduardo, Maurice, Bessi,* and *Leonard,* to name a few, were written in script or printed within elements of the design. Some of the names were easy to spot, others you had to look for. Occasionally the Pucci-like fashions popped up on eBay and they were selling for decent prices. I started to purchase them myself. At the time, I was able to pick up a nice *Paganne* or *Mr. Dino* dress for less than fifty dollars, a *Bessi* or *Leonard of Paris* cost more, and a real *Pucci* print was a couple of hundred dollars. Today, the prices have escalated to the hundreds for some of the knock-off prints and to the thousands for rare vintage Pucci prints. As my collection grew, I would stare at the dresses that seemed to speak to me. Their fabrics were luxurious, especially the silk jersey that Emilio Pucci and Averardo Bessi used and that Daniel Tribouillard used for Leonard of Paris. Dresses signed *Mr. Dino* and *Maurice* were usually made of nylon jersey or other synthetics that looked and felt almost as soft as the more expensive fabrics and still had the appeal of more expensive dresses but had prices that were somewhat less. Prints signed *Eduardo* were usually lounging robes, pajamas, hostess gowns, or nightgowns. They were mostly made of new nylons that were produced by textile manufacturers throughout the nineteen-sixties.

I later learned that some of the allure of these dresses was that they appealed to jet-setters of the nineteen sixties and seventies. A printed silk jersey dress designed by Emilio Pucci, for instance, weighed about three or four ounces. An avid traveler going to a resort destination could pack a half dozen or more dresses into one suitcase, and when they were unpacked they were virtually wrinkle-free. Since celebrities, actresses, and high-society people were photographed wearing Pucci prints; working girls who admired these people could afford the luxury of buying a knock-off or imitation Pucci print. This made a huge impact on textile manufacturers, fabric designers, and fashion designers, as well as consumers. Advances in the textiles field gave manufacturers fabrics that were tested for durability as well as packability. The jet-age was here to stay, and travelers from all walks of life were dressing like the rich and famous. A signature in a print became a status symbol. For more than a decade, bold, bright, and sometimes complex prints with designers' signatures were thoroughly enjoyed by women from all walks of life. Today, there are more signature print fashions waiting to be uncovered.

INTRODUCTION

The jet age of the 20th century encompassed much more than advances in aircraft. After World War II, international aviation was responsible for a close relationship with the fashion world. Exotic lands were being visited, different cultures were being observed, and fashion was changing to suit the needs of jet-setters who traveled from coast to coast as well as climate to climate. Jet travel, beginning around 1958 with the use of the Boeing 707 and Lockeed L188 Turboprop jetliners, brought people and places closer together.

The fashion clothing industry changed with the help of BOAC (British Overseas Airways Corporation), now British Airways, which was the first airline to offer a new service to its travelers, information regarding preferable types of clothing to pack and the right fabrics to choose for a particular destination. This service, called the Travel Fashion Advisory Service, provided packing lists for worldwide locations and their corresponding climates. It gave lists for both First Class and Economy Service baggage allowances.

Advances in jet air travel inspired fashion clothing designers, who picked up on their growing trend to attract customers and their creativity abounded. Resort wear fashions were geared for exotic beaches at Nassau, Bermuda, and Jamaica. Hollywood's regulars enjoyed the popular resort town of Acapulco, Mexico. New York jet-setters enjoyed Palm Beach, Florida. In 1960, it took only four hours to fly from New York to Jamaica; seven hours from New York to Paris; and ten hours from New York to Rome. Flying to Bali, Indonesia, and the Orient became commonplace among designers, celebrities and members of high society who thought nothing of flying to Rome, London, or Paris for a weekend to attend a party or an event. Their clothing had to travel well. It was not the days when ocean liners could take huge steamer trunks filled with clothing that needed to be pressed or steamed, and you brought your maid or butler on the trip with you. The new international jet-setters were on the move and raring to go.

One designer who played a strategic role in new fashions for the travelers was Emilio Pucci. As early as the late 1950s, his silk printed blouses and pants "literally swept the fashion scene in Jamaica and Florida," according to *American Fabrics*. His clothing designs also were popular and being worn by tourists in Palm Beach and Montego Bay. This direction in resort wear was the impetus for the overall "Pucci-mania" that evolved throughout the 1960s and early 1970s. Emilio Pucci's silk jersey dresses created an international sensation. Weighing only three or four ounces, glamorous day dresses and evening gowns of silk jersey could be packed into a suitcase and taken out after a flight virtually wrinkle-free. This sat well with people traveling on a regular basis. What was even better was that Pucci silk prints could be packed in a carry-on suitcase and be ready to wear upon arrival. Pucci silk dresses, gowns, palazzo pants, and blouses were quite expensive when they were first introduced, and that encouraged many copycat designers to followed his lead throughout the 1960s and create their own prints, that sold for around $9.98 for an off-the-rack style.

Emilio Pucci, in collaboration with interior designer Alexander Girard, was approached by Dallas-based Braniff International Airlines, in 1965, to redesign the clothing worn by their in-flight and ground crews and to recolor the interiors and exteriors of their planes. This promotion was intended to make air travel with Braniff more glamorous. Girard colored the insides and outsides of the jetliners in one of seven hues, ranging from bright orange to turquoise. Pucci created flight crew uniforms that he called the "QC," which stood for "quick change," so that during a single flight stewardesses could have four different clothing looks. They ranged from a now-famous, plastic dome hat, called the Gemini space helmet, with matching boots and gloves, to a printed wrap-around skirt to be worn with boots or pumps, to printed culottes worn with a turtle-neck top and flat shoes, and finally to a serving dress in a two-toned print called a "Puccino," which, of course, was made from wash-and-wear fabric. Pucci created several different lines from 1965 to 1974, when fashion designer Halston took over the job as Braniff's uniform designer.

Pucci's signature fashions inspired later designs by Bessi, Leonard, Pulitzer, Shaheen, Mr. Dino, Paganne, and a host of others.

Braniff International Airways "Jet Age" Lockheed L188 Turbo-prop Jetliner, circa 1959.

Hostess uniforms designed by Emilio Pucci for Braniff International Airways. The Gemini IV collection in 1965 consisted of the Space Bubble helmet inspired by NASA. The plastic bubble-shaped hat was perfect for keeping the hostesses hair protected from inclement weather but did not stay in fashion very long as it proved to be unrealistic. It was only used for one year, making it extremely rare today! The Pucci II collection in 1966 featured multi-colored printed tunics and matching leotards. This print was called "Ports of Call" as it recognized all of the different nations that Braniff International served.

> *During the years of his ascendancy, Pucci not only made a fortune for himself but also for the countless manufacturers who copied and imitated his prints.*
> **Stanley Marcus,** 1974

By the early 1970s, dynamic prints designed by Emilio Pucci, the "founding father of the signature print," were beginning to take a back seat for travelers to denim jeans and t-shirts, granny dresses, and polyester pants suits. Around that same time, the excitement for colorful clothes that had been prevalent for so many years began to wane. The glitter and sparkle of disco, hot pants, platform shoes, and leisure suits were being worn by another generation of young people who looked at fashion not as jet-set glamour but as hip, trendy and funky. Swank discotheques like New York's Studio 54 was the new destination for anyone who was anyone wanting to be seen. The world was changing, but there were serious Pucci fanatics who never lost interest in Pucci designs. A revival of his styles occurred in the 1980s, and again in the 1990s. The 21st century brought renewed interest in designs by Emilio Pucci once more.

As early as 1963, these "loose-fitting silk shifts" with wonderful and colorful prints became "Pucci best sellers". *Ladies' Home Journal*, July-August, 1963

A simple design with a catchy print was Pucci's recipe for success. This belted shift weighed only four ounces and was popular with jet setters in the early sixties. *Ladies' Home Journal*, July-August, 1963

AREMIS

In the late sixties and early seventies, major department stores stocked their designer boutiques with haute couture. The rage for clothing designed by Emilio Pucci was overwhelming. Right alongside the real thing were "Pucci-esque" fashions that appealed to the working girl on a lesser budget who could not afford the luxury of owning a silk jersey dress designed by an Italian marchese. Because of the high demand, knock-off artists or copycat designers manufactured similar styles using less expensive fabrics and even added a signature to the ubiquitous print. This evening gown with a dynamic print rendered in a wonderful color palette is signed *Aremis.* Certain aspects of this design can be found in authentic Pucci prints. Double-strand necklace and earring set rendered in pastel-colored beads stamped Japan. Four-strand glass and rhinestone bracelet with jeweled clasp by DeMario.

Close-up of Aremis signature strategically placed in the print.

Notice the Aremis signature on the leaf.

Today women expect their clothes to be comfortable, packable, easy to care for; at the same time, they want them to be luxurious and fashion-right. It's the supple stretch knits that fit the bill.
American Fabrics, Summer, 1966

Maxi-dress with fitted silhouette and whimsical floral theme signed Aremis. Large enameled pendant necklace with oriental motif, unmarked. Jewel-tipped dangle earrings in rhodium-plated metal. This emerald-cut faux citrine ring is contemporary.

The silk fabrics Emilio Pucci has been using for his famous shifts have been out of the price reach of most American consumers. In a way, it has been a pity, because this uncluttered, sexy and comfortable dress is an exciting fashion to most young American women. However, a short while ago – through a strong assist from the newly developed tri-global Antron nylon cloths – this silk-like dress began to be available to a far wider audience.
American Fabrics, Summer, 1963

"Pucci-esque" sleeveless gown of Antron nylon with fitted bodice and decorative banding. The abstract print is rendered in a multitude of psychedelic colors. Numerous Aremis signatures are found throughout the print and the dress is labeled Aremis, Made in Italy.

Opposite page:
Salmon-colored faux fur jacket labeled Jobere by Morty Sussman. Demi-parure consisting of a choker necklace and matching bracelet made of glass and plastic beads with cascading centerpieces. Although the jewelry is not signed, it is similar to the work of Miriam Haskell or Robert DeMario. Molded pale pink plastic rose ring accented with rhinestones in a gold-plated setting.

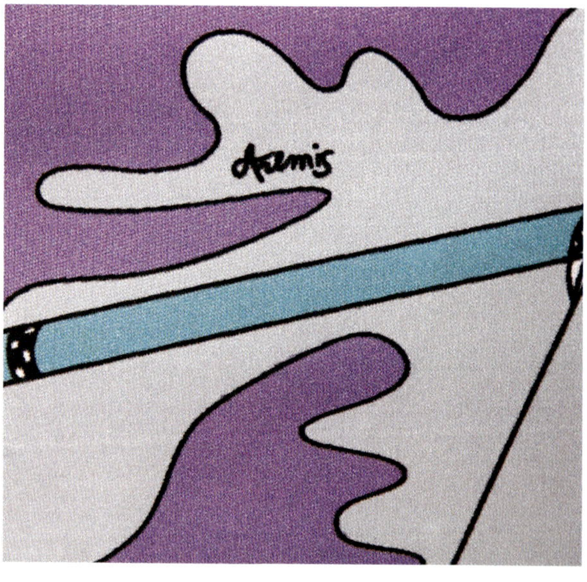

Close-up of the Aremis signature found in the print.

ARTEMIS

Stretch knit chemise with a four-toned geometric print accented in black and signed Artemis. Due to the tremendous success that Emilio Pucci achieved throughout the sixties, copycat designers and knock-off artists flourished and the volume market was more than ready to accept anything that closely resembled a print designed by an Italian nobleman. Propelled by the desire to look as good as the elite at a fraction of the cost, these Pucci-esque fashions were plentiful for more than a decade. Available in a wide assortment of synthetic fabrics, the prints were bursting with color; the designs were becoming complex; and they all sported a signature or numerous signatures found in the prints. Pink patent leather pumps by J.Renee.

Emilio Pucci was the most copied designer of our time aside from Chanel.
Stanley Marcus (president of Neiman-Marcus stores), 1974

Articulated pave' rhinestone drop earrings enhanced with faux pearls by Bellini. Rhinestone encrusted bracelet with double leopard design by Ciner. Large faceted clear crystal and rhinestone pendant necklace suspended from a fine rhinestone chain signed Miriam Haskell. Close-up of the Artemis signature found near the banded border at the sleeve.

Close-up of the Artemis signature in the print and the grain on the leather handbag.

Chemise designed with a drop waist reminiscent of an Art Deco era flapper dress. The sinuous print, on the other hand, is suggestive of the Art Nouveau era. The dress is signed Artemis. A thin bright orange leather handbag with a pebble grain effect has been fitted with a chain handle. Open-toe sling back heels made of clear Lucite and spotted and dyed fur by Joseph.

Gold-plated choker necklace with adjustable chain and huge flower pendant accented with clear pave' rhinestones. Demi-parure consisting of segmented bracelet and clip earrings designed with large dome-shaped faceted amber glass stones and aurora borealis rhinestones, unmarked.

The lid's off in prints! Imagination and daring – combined with a flair for colors – have focused the fashion world's attention in the direction of prints.
American Fabrics, Summer, 1966

Long sleeve printed chemise signed and labeled Artemis. Notice the different motifs in the print and the banding at the cuffs and hemline. The dress has an obvious Art Deco flair. Metallic leather heels with ankle ties by Polly Bergen.

Space age chrome and plastic pendant necklace, unmarked. Chrome and faceted blue glass segmented bracelet, accented with rhinestones, also unmarked.

Close-up of the Artemis signature discreetly hidden in the print.

BESSI

Spectacular two-pieced silk evening gown with sheer over blouse labeled Bessi, Firenze, Italia. Notice how the stand-up collar and cuffs on the sheer over blouse match the printed banding on the gown. Blue peau de soie shoes by Charles Jourdan, Paris.

Gorgeous parure of lavender crystal beads enhanced with ornate filigree, crystal and rhinestone clusters. Although the parure is unmarked, it is very much like the work of Robert DeMario. How many Bessi signatures can you find?

Bessi gown without the sheer over blouse. Notice how the banding accentuates every aspect of this dress thus taming down the wild print to create sophistication.

Averardo Bessi founded his company in 1950 in Italy. Being a contemporary of Emilio Pucci, Bessi also worked with the finest silk jersey and wonderful velvets. He designed prints similar to Pucci as well as designing others that were unique to his own style. Many of his prints were abstracts, geometrics and florals in vibrant hues and wonderful color combinations. He also designed many prints with a palette of pastel colors. Bessi signed his prints. The earlier vintage prints were signed with the name *Bessi* while the later fashions and accessories have the full name of *Averardo Bessi* hidden in the print. Bessi apparel was sold in high end department stores like Bonwit Teller and Bergdorf Goodman. The Italian company is still in existence today selling exquisite high end fashions and complete ensembles made of the finest fabrics.

Hand-manipulated Lucite and hand blown glass beaded and fringed neckpiece creating a three-dimensional effect. Although this gorgeous necklace is not signed, it is similar to the work of Mimi di N. Pink translucent and aurora borealis rhinestone earrings. The model also is wearing the matching bracelet. Notice the Bessi signature on the right shoulder.

Close-up of the Averardo Bessi signature found in the floral print.

Opposite page:
Pure silk jersey chemise with flared bottom and banded borders signed Bessi. The dress was made in Italy for Bonwit Teller. Italian leather peep toe pumps with cutout decorations and lace-up ankle ties by Cities.

The skyrocketing airline stocks which have been the talk of the New York Stock Exchange these recent months seem to emphasize once again the fact that we are living in an age of travel. The fashion industry has known this for a long time and the unspoken question in making up a line is "Will it travel well?"
American Fabrics, Summer, 1964

Classic printed silk jersey chemise with banding around the neckline, cuffs and hemline. The dress is signed Averardo Bessi and labeled Bessi, Firenze, Italia. The luxurious silk jersey fabric was desirable for many reasons among the jet setters. Packability was high on their list. Oversized Lucite layered and fringed necklace by Tatiana, Italy; Lucite and goldtone mules by Frederick's of Hollywood.

Closer view of the faceted citrine bead and filigree choker necklace accented with citrine-colored rhinestones by unknown maker. Pave' rhinestone panther ring signed Panetta.

Silk chiffon dress with fitted waist, banded borders and sheer bell sleeves signed Bessi and labeled Bessi, Firenze, Italia. Italian leather peep toe pumps with ankle ties by Cities.

Goldtone bamboo pendant necklace by Napier. Jeweled and enameled hinged bangle bracelet by K.J.L. Grecian-inspired gold-plated chain belt with lion head medallions, unmarked.

Cotton velvet pants with a funky cloud print rendered in psychedelic colors and signed Bessi. Gold metallic leather and jeweled wedgies labeled Caparros; bright yellow vinyl tote bag with zippered front pocket, unmarked.

Close-up of the Bessi signature and jeweled wedgies.

DON MANUEL

Large pendant necklace designed with a molded plastic scarab mounted in a textured gold-plated setting signed K.J.L. Genuine Lucite bangle bracelets in bright red, royal blue and canary yellow.

Closer view of the Don Manuel signature accompanied by a copyright symbol and positioned under the fleur de lis pattern.

Button-down shirt-dress with a classic Baroque pattern signed Don Manuel and labeled Don Manuel of Miami. Spike heel shoes made of gold and silver Mylar threads by Joyce, California.

EDUARDO

This zip-front robe with Art Nouveau style print was rendered in pretty pastel colors. It is signed Eduardo and labeled Saks Fifth Avenue, Young Dimensions. Two-toned leather platform heels were designed by Charles Jourdan, Paris. The wide pave' rhinestone bracelet has no identifying marks.

Hostess gowns, nightgowns, palazzo pajamas, robes and ensembles made of nylon with wild and wonderful prints signed Eduardo can be found today at auction and vintage clothing boutiques. Certain Eduardo labels read Saks Fifth Avenue, Young Dimensions; others read Travel-Lite by Boutique. Regardless of the label, the Pucci-style print was signed Eduardo and cost less than the real thing! They were desirable enough to be sold in fine department stores at a fraction of the cost of a real Pucci print because the demand was so high. The impetus for these exciting prints in sleepwear came from Pucci's "Suitcase Shift" which was advertised in 1967 as packable, *practical, as non-wrinkle-able as any travel nightie you've ever owned.* They were designed by Emilio Pucci as travel sleepwear and made by Formfit Rogers.

Now twenty-one years old, nylon has long ceased to be simply a functional utility fiber. It now occupies a secure place in the world of fashion and its future is full of promise.
American Fabrics, Winter, 1961-62

Opposite page:
Nylon nightgown with zip front and floral print rendered in psychedelic colors signed Eduardo. The metallic purple leather mules were designed by Maud Frizon, Paris. Long necklace made of multi-strand plastic beads in shades of pink and purple, unmarked. Plastic studded earrings and matching bangle bracelet by Accessocraft.

Close-up of the Eduardo signature and the rhinestone-studded plastic bangle bracelet.

Nylon zip-front nightgown signed Eduardo and labeled Travel-Lite by Boutique. Lariat-style necklace and earring set of faceted white plastic beads and goldtone metal, unmarked; black and gold slippers by Daniel Green.

Nylon zip-front hostess gown or robe with Pucci style geometric print executed in psychedelic colors. The robe is signed Eduardo and labeled Saks Fifth Avenue. Deep purple metallic leather mules designed by Maud Frizon, Paris.

Twisted tendrils of yellow and purple plastic were used to create oversized mod earrings by an unknown maker. Draped triple-strand necklace designed with three shades of graduated and faceted genuine Lucite accented with goldtone spacers. Trio of canary yellow bangle bracelets made of genuine DuPont Lucite.

Close-up of the Eduardo signature positioned in the Pucci-esque print.

Silk polka dot signature scarf signed Leo Narducci. Jeweled and enameled hinged bracelet made by Boucher; blue and white polka dot bead necklace, unmarked.

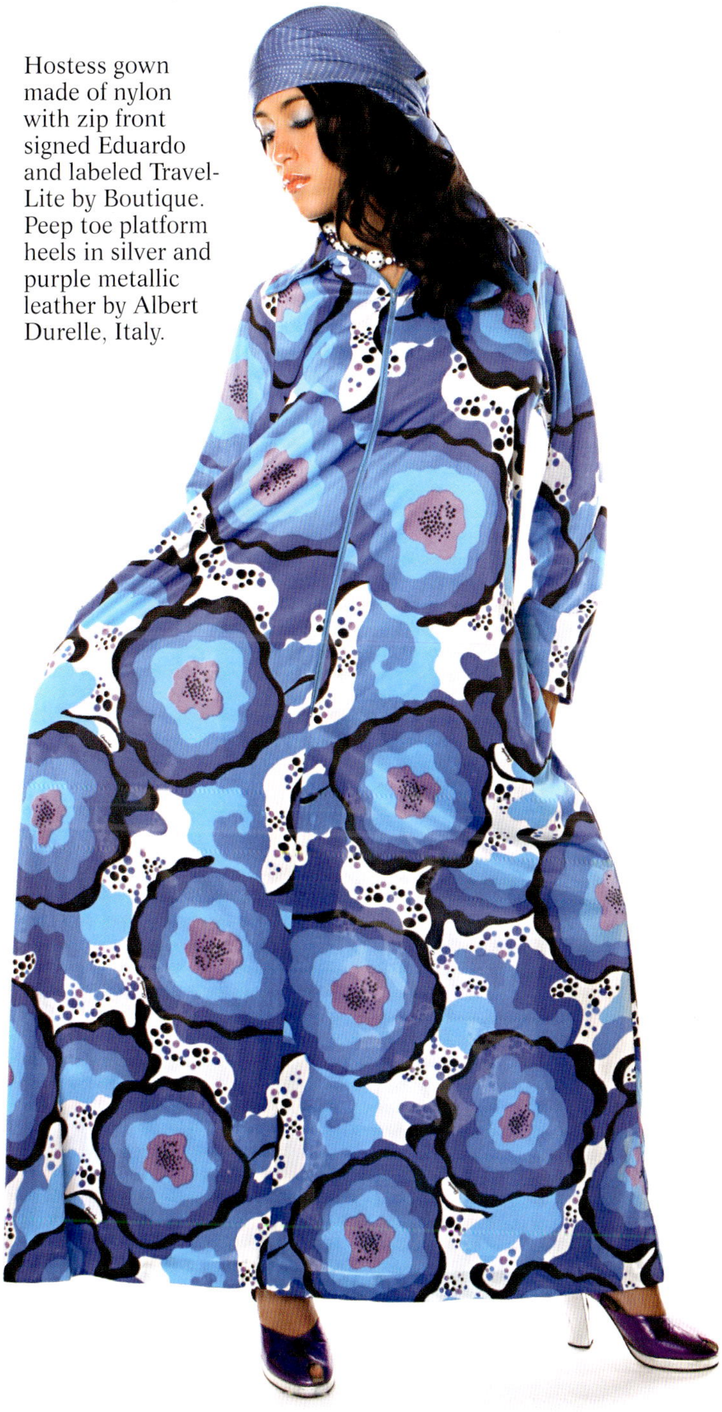

Hostess gown made of nylon with zip front signed Eduardo and labeled Travel-Lite by Boutique. Peep toe platform heels in silver and purple metallic leather by Albert Durelle, Italy.

Eduardo signature discreetly found in the busy print.

Prints have the enduring quality of uniqueness. A woman may express her public self in other patterns; she expresses her private self in prints, thus, their lasting appeal.
American Fabrics, Spring, 1968

Taking a closer look at this hinged bracelet and matching earring set, the large faceted rhinestones emit a rainbow of color. The faux pearls further enhance this unmarked demi-parure.

Floral nightgown made of nylon labeled Travel-Lite by Boutique. The floral print is signed Eduardo. Gold leather peep toe sling backs by Andrea Pfister.

A closer look at the Eduardo signature in the print. I wonder how many people were fooled back in the sixties with this signature since it also began with an "E" and was done in black script like Emilio. I am sure that it fooled quite a few! Goldtone and white enameled link bracelet manufactured by Coro.

Intended for at-home wear, this one-piece jumpsuit, made of nylon, is signed Eduardo and labeled Saks Fifth Avenue. Cotton printed scarf signed Emilio and labeled Emilio Pucci. The gold metallic slippers with the fluffy pom-poms were made by Daniel Green. Large fringed neckpiece made of gold-plated metal and white beads, unmarked.

EMILIO PUCCI

Silk jersey flapper-style dress with v-neckline, Empire waist, banded borders and silken fringe at the hemline. The dress is signed Emilio and labeled Emilio Pucci, Florence, Italy. Choker necklace of silvertone metal with a large floral medallion is unmarked. Black suede ankle strap heels by Premiere Collection.

Prints that catch the eye and make an immediate impact seem to have a life of movement all their own.
American Fabrics, Winter-Spring, 1967

A closer view of the luxurious silk fringed hem and four Emilio signatures. Jeweled high-heeled sandals made by Valerie Stevens.

Known as the "Prince of Prints" and the "Founding Father of the Signature Print," Emilio Pucci had the right idea at just the right time. When World War II ended, the buying public had a desire for anything but drab clothing. Pucci was also born into an aristocratic Florentine family. He was on a ski team at Reed College in Portland, Oregon, in the 1930s, and at that time designed the ski uniforms for the team. As an Italian war hero, he attended American colleges and received an M.A. in social science and a Ph.D. in political science from the University of Florence. Pucci's career as a fashion designer began as a fluke in 1948. Skiing the Swiss Alps, Pucci was spotted by Toni Frissell, a photographer for *Harper's Bazaar*, wearing smart looking ski clothes that he had designed himself. The pictures taken by Frissell were shown in the December 1948 issue of *Harper's Bazaar*. Lord & Taylor placed an order for his ski clothes, which White Stag then manufactured.

Pucci spent summers on the island of Capri and was inspired to create a wardrobe for a pretty woman that he met on the island. His inspiration by the island and the Mediterranean atmosphere made his creativity emerge like the dawn of a new day. With the help of a local dress maker, Pucci began creating some really unique outfits which immediately caught the eye of those vacationing on the island, including some wealthy Americans. Before long, Pucci opened a boutique on Capri and then another in Rome. He opened workrooms in his rundown palazzo in Florence, Italy. His collections became known as *Emilio* and were shown at the first Italian fashion show in 1951. Emilio Pucci was actually more of an artist than a designer. He created brilliant prints with striking color combinations that were virtually impossible to duplicate. Many knock-off artists, copycat designers and manufacturers tried to imitate Emilio Pucci's creations but no one actually came close. Pucci decided to sign his prints with the name *Emilio* knowing that even though his prints were being copied, no one could actually copy his name.

By 1950, Pucci was becoming increasingly well-known. The American press called him *Emilio of Capri* and his resort wear was filling boutiques in major department stores across America. Early in his career, Pucci designed silk squares with unusual prints. On a buying trip to Florence in 1948, Stanley Marcus of the Dallas-based Neiman-Marcus department store met Emilio Pucci and placed a small order of his silk scarves. Marcus encouraged Pucci to possibly make blouses or even dresses out of the silk printed squares. Pucci began making his scarf blouse and then coordinating them with solid color stretch "Capri" pants. They became an important part of every socialite's wardrobe visiting resort locations around the globe. Silk printed shifts followed and then his famous silk jersey dresses with the most powerful prints imaginable. The buying public was not only fascinated with his prints but also the fact that these prints were designed by an Italian marchese. Pucci prints became a status symbol and famous celebrities and royalty were spotted wearing Pucci clothes. Ingrid Bergman, Elizabeth Taylor, Connie Francis, Gina Lollobrigida and Marilyn Monroe, to name a few wore Pucci prints. Socialites skiing St. Moritz in winter or lying on the beach in Acapulco in summer were spotted wearing Pucci clothes. From Palm Beach to Palm Springs, the "in-crowd" wore Pucci. The luxurious fabrics, especially the silk jersey tube dresses, gained instantaneous popularity with the international jet set traveling from coast to coast as well as from one climate to another. A Pucci silk jersey tube dress weighed only about four ounces. It could travel well and was easy to care for. Unfortunately for the average working girl, Pucci silk jersey dresses were expensive when they were first introduced and out of their reach. This was one of the main reasons that Pucci prints were being copied so readily. Also, authentic Pucci dresses, being so desirable, were often shoplifted from major department stores in high percentages. Women were fascinated with the kaleidoscope of prints that Pucci designed. The buying public was hungry for prints; Puccimania was overwhelming. If one couldn't purchase an authentic Pucci then a pseudo-pucci print would have to do.

> *Think of the Victorian family portrait - the woman laced in corsets, the man starched and stiff. Then think of a young girl in a miniskirt striding confidently down the avenue. There is the difference. Today's fashion is one with the body, essentially natural and simple, the flow of the fabric expressing the movement of the body, freed of inhibitions.*
> Emilio Pucci, 1968

Close-up of two of the many Emilio signatures found in the print. The glamorous bib necklace with matching drop earrings was made of clear and fuchsia-colored rhinestones, unmarked. Clamper bracelet set with clear rhinestones in rhodium-plated metal, also unmarked.

Close-up of the Emilio signature found on the Pucci silk tie.

A closer look at the signature print lining found in this handsome Emilio Pucci jacket.

Navy blue double-breasted wool sport jacket with signature print lining labeled Emilio Pucci by Ermenegildo Zegna, Tailored in Italy, Saks Fifth Avenue.

Front and back view of Pucci silk jersey zip-front shift dress with drop waist accented with banded borders. The banding separates the diagonal print from the harlequin print.. The overall appeal is a touch of Art Nouveau and an exceptional color palette. Multi-colored leather pumps by Martinez Valero.

Italy has given the Art Nouveau approach a new twist by combining flowers, ribbons and medallions in many printed fabrics.
American Fabrics, Winter-Spring, 1964

Spectacular oversized citrine rhinestone pendant necklace suspended from rhinestone chain by Schreiner. Close-up of the Emilio signature found in the print.

Inspiration for his prints came from varied sources. Emilio Pucci was an avid traveler who loved to visit exotic lands like Bali, Indonesia and Africa. South America and the Aztec influence were also inspiring to this Florentine aristocrat. He was also inspired by the island of Capri and other islands in the Mediterranean as well as his own Florentine surroundings. Medieval influences were evident in his late 1950s "Palio" collection when his designs were reminiscent of the heraldic banners of the 12th century. Geometry entered the scene in the early sixties after his trips to Indonesia and Africa. More geometrics and Art Deco motifs came into play with his most popular line "Vivara" line in 1966. Archeological ruins, sculpture and Renaissance art were also important to this Florentine aristocrat who was said to have become a millionaire by 1952 and by 1963, the richest fashion designer in the world.

From the standpoint of pleasant body contact, few fabrics equal fine jersey, which is a fabric that the skin loves to touch! Consequently, fine jersey has always had great appeal for both men and women, as well as being an ideal young world fashion fabric. Washable, crease-resistant, packable, this new jersey will have a great appeal for the jet set which expects a built in valet with every purchase!
American Fabrics, Summer, 1965

Bracelet made of clear Lucite and black glass seed beads signed Miriam Haskell. Clear rhinestone encrusted sphere suspended from a rhinestone chain, unmarked. Four Emilio signatures are visible in this section of the bodice.

Emilio Pucci's designs were a breath of fresh air. Postwar Americans were open for new and exciting directions in the world of fashion. Casual sportswear and less rigid dress clothes were becoming increasingly popular. Italian fashion designers were coming into the forefront. Parisian designers and haute couture was now taking a back seat. Pucci's creations were cleverly assimilated into a society that was devastated by war. Pucci managed to restore the family's palazzo and his collections were shown in the regal atmosphere of a centuries old palazzo. Before long, Pucci designs were encompassing a whole new realm of products and the name Pucci became synonymous with high fashion, lingerie, perfume, jewelry, handbags, towels, bedding, porcelain, sunglasses, carpets, lithographs, cars, motorcycles and a host of other products bearing the *Emilio* name. "Puccimania" was everywhere. He created a casual elegance that has classic appeal. Emilio Pucci became an icon in the 20th century and now, more than ever, his vintage signature prints are highly prized in the 21st century.

Pucci sleeveless silk jersey dress with scoop neckline, Empire waist, geometric print bodice and solid black skirt. The signature Emilio is found numerous times in this print. Black suede ankle strap heels by Premiere Collection.

Artist rendering of an Emilio Pucci two-piece silk jersey outfit with a lovely scarf print as advertised in Vogue in 1964 for Lord & Taylor. This outfit retailed for $145.00 at that time. This was a promotional ad to create interest in Italian designers. The magazine ad campaign also made reference to Elizabeth Arden's Pablo who was a make-up designer for the Elizabeth Arden Salon in Rome. Interest for all things Italian was extremely hot at that time.

Authentic Pucci harem pajamas might be lacking the print but not the pizzazz! The outfit was accessorized with exceptional Mimi di N jewelry. *Ladies' Home Journal*, December, 1966

Prints have become as much a fashion force as Famous People and Famous Designers. They sweep over all the barriers – mighty oceans, broad rivers, and the highest barrier of all in women's wear, the Almighty Season. Prints have become nearly seasonless!
American Fabrics, Spring, 1969

Large silvertone coiled wire pendant necklace and matching earrings, unmarked. Two blue mirrored Lucite bangle bracelets by unknown maker.

Opposite page:
Fringed chemise made of silk jersey with a captivating engineered print rendered in wonderful psychedelic colors and signed Emilio. Notice the uniqueness of each side of the dress due in part by the positioning of the banded borders. These dresses were also referred to as tube dresses but without the added silk fringe. The foot flattering silk ribbon heels were designed by Gucci, Made in Italy.

Silk jersey mini-dress designed by Emilio Pucci as well as the woven rug made of silky wool featuring the same print as the dress in a different color combination. The rugs were made in Argentina by a company known as Dandolo y Primi. The rug is also signed Emilio. *Domenica del Corriere*, 1971

Opposite page:
Front and back view of Pucci silk jersey flapper style chemise with pink silk fringed hem. The harlequin print is signed Emilio. Peep toe sling back peau de soie heels accented with clear crystals by Charles Jourdan, Paris. White beaded necklace with rose motif in pink by Lanvin, Paris. Drop earrings by Monet.

Close-up of Emilio signature on banding at neckline. White Lucite dome ring made in the mod style of the sixties.

The Harlequin trend has come to the fore during the past few months on the French and Italian Riviera. In all types of fabric, the Harlequin theme showed up best in color combinations away from the trite and ordinary. Dior pioneered this trend a couple of seasons ago by scoring a smash hit with black and white diamonds shot with color. While Harlequin is associated with the character Pierrot, the design theme has something reminiscent of Americana, especially in many of the early American samplers and needlepoint creations.
American Fabrics, Winter, 1961-62

A clever combination of ebony wood, faux pearls, plastic beads and sculpted leather flowers were utilized to create this oversized, three-dimensional fringed neckpiece by unknown maker. Black plastic bangle bracelet enhanced with clear rhinestones by Accessocraft. Check out the Emilio signature positioned at the shoulder.

Pucci silk jersey mini-dress with fitted waist, full skirt and banding. The awesome print has many Emilio signatures. Skin tight boots made of black spandex, no label.

Pucci silk jersey over blouse and matching palazzo pants with an abstract vertical striped print rendered in psychedelic colors. The outfit is labeled Emilio Pucci, Florence, Italy, Exclusively for Saks Fifth Avenue. Hot pink patent leather pumps by J. Renee.

Close-up of Emilio signatures in the print. Bib necklace and earring set made of green plastic beads suspended from a chain link background. A glitzy clamper-style bracelet is set with clear rhinestones and faux emeralds in a gold-plated setting.

Opposite page:
Pucci v-neck tunic top and matching maxi skirt made of luxurious silk jersey with a stark geometric print rendered in a deep color palette. The bold geometrics are echoed by a more subdued print in the border design. Unique slip-on mules designed with four different colors of leather forming a stylized bow by Beverly Feldman.

Unusual fringed necklace and matching drop earrings, maker unknown. Large brass filigree ring set with faux gemstones, also unmarked. Close-up of the vivid Pucci print and a few Emilio signatures.

The great Cubist period in art which took the world by storm earlier in this century is still exerting an influence on today's designs. Many of the newest prints are derived from cubes and other geometric forms which painters like Picasso, Braque and Delaunay used to explore new realms in color and form. There prints are faintly reminiscent of those we associate with Pucci fabrics, which continue to please present-day print connoisseurs. Done in fresh 1967 color combinations, these "cubist" prints have contemporary appeal which makes them important in the world of prints. **American Fabrics,** Winter-Spring, 1967

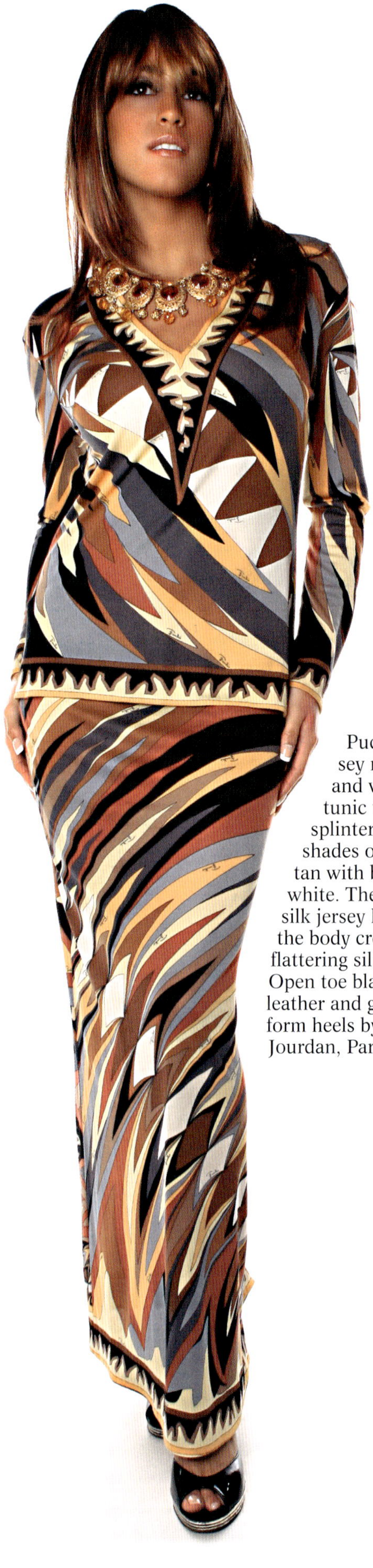

Pucci silk jersey maxi skirt and v-neck tunic top with splinter print in shades of brown, tan with black and white. The luxurious silk jersey hugged the body creating a flattering silhouette. Open toe black patent leather and gold platform heels by Charles Jourdan, Paris.

Exceptional Middle Eastern style neckpiece made of gold-plated filigree medallions accented with large topaz glass stones and drops, unmarked. Topaz crystal cluster earrings, also unmarked. Numerous Emilio signatures are visible in this eye-popping print.

Suddenly, the fashion world is geometry conscious. The symbols of mathematics hold a special fascination for young females who would never dream of taking courses in higher math or physics. Geometry in fashion means the squares, circles, triangles – all elegant symbols introduced by Euclid himself. They take on new zest when presented in zingy contemporary colors and in unexpected, dynamic arrangements.
American Fabrics, Summer, 1966

Close-up of the Emilio signatures found in the geometric print. Huge textured gold-plated neckpiece accented with faux amethyst beads and long metal fringe. The chain is also enhanced with the amethyst glass beads. Wide purple Lucite bangle bracelet accented with brass studs by Accessocraft.

1960s vintage silk jersey chemise with geometric print rendered in vibrant hues designed by Emilio Pucci. Banded borders outline the v-neck, sleeves, hem line and down the back of the dress. Tan leather open toe ankle straps with open wedge heel in black by Charles Jourdan, Paris.

The word look is on everybody's tongue these days. Taste varies, and fortunately there are many looks, representing enough variety of silhouettes to allow every woman her rightful choice. Among the promising candidates for fashion honors with many women in the silhouette which can be termed "the long lean look." It's particularly flattering for the so-called American figure, world-famous for its legs. This look has certain innocence and also paradoxically, a certain seductive air.

American Fabrics, Summer, 1963

Pucci two-piece ensemble designed for evening wear. The outfit consists of a tailored semi-sheer silk blouse and a lined maxi skirt with a wonderful abstract print in shades of lilac, periwinkle, raspberry, gray, black and white. Emilio Pucci was a master colorist and many tried to imitate his intricate prints but very few even came close to his exceptional creations. A legion of copycats tried, however, during the print parade of the sixties and early seventies. Periwinkle leather and Lucite ankle tie shoes by Gamins, Spain.

Opposite page:
Casual elegance can describe this cotton printed blouse and palazzo pants ensemble with one of Emilio Pucci's most desirable prints.

Closer view of the Pucci silk blouse with the wonderful abstract print. Notice again the creative used of banding in this silhouette. Multi-strand draped necklace composed of assorted baubles, beads and chain. Large pewter-colored faux pearl earrings are unmarked.

Close-up of the rosebud print revealing numerous Emilio signatures. Turquoise leather shoes by Bonnie Smith for Kimmel.

Fringed necklace composed of turquoise plastic drops suspended from a goldtone chain. Turquoise thermoplastic drop earrings accented with clear rhinestones. The oversized faux turquoise ring in heavy gold-plated setting is unmarked.

Front and back view of striking Pucci silk jersey evening gown with a wonderful geometric print and a sexy fitted silhouette. Notice the creative use of banding which is echoed in the stand-up collar. The large pendant necklace made of square-cut faux amethyst stones is unmarked. Wide hinged bracelet encrusted with amethyst-colored stones and faux pearls, also unmarked. Black suede sling-backs by Via Spiga, Italy.

Side view of Pucci silk jersey gown revealing three Emilio signatures on the banding down the side of the sleeve. Also a closer look at the glorious bejeweled bracelet fit for a queen! The amethyst crystal cluster earrings are unmarked.

Another version of the coveted Pucci rosebud print, this time in cotton velvet and made into a cropped jacket and matching maxi skirt. Emilio Pucci generated fashion drama with his spectacular prints and choice of colors. This eye-popping color palette screams the sixties! Bright orange patent leather pumps by J.Renee.

Faux turquoise necklace with clear pave' rhinestone enhancer further accented with a turquoise glass drop. Turquoise glass and clear rhinestone drop earrings signed Bellini.

Fringed necklace made with faux pearls and blue faceted glass beads suspended from a chunky gold-plated chain. Drop earrings of goldtone filigree set with aurora borealis rhinestones. Gold-plated dome ring set with clear rhinestones; black patent leather and glitter pumps made by Imperial.

During the 14th and 15th centuries, Italy became the great European center for velvet manufacture and the cities of Lucca, Genoa, Florence and Venice achieved world renown for the richness and unsurpassed luxury of their ornamented velvets. The word velvet itself comes for the Italian velluto. **American Fabrics**, Spring-Summer, 1962

Pucci two-piece outfit with semi-sheer silk chiffon blouse and velvet palazzo pants. Again, the rosebud print is repeated and rendered in shades of purple and turquoise on a black background.

Front and back view of Pucci long sleeve cashmere tube dress with multi-colored geometric engineered print. Notice how the dress takes on an entirely different look with the continuous banding in the back. Purple suede shoes by Trosconini.

Close-up of the Emilio signature in the banding on the v-neckline. Lucite beaded necklace made in shades of blue with clear fluted beads and silvertone filigree accents.

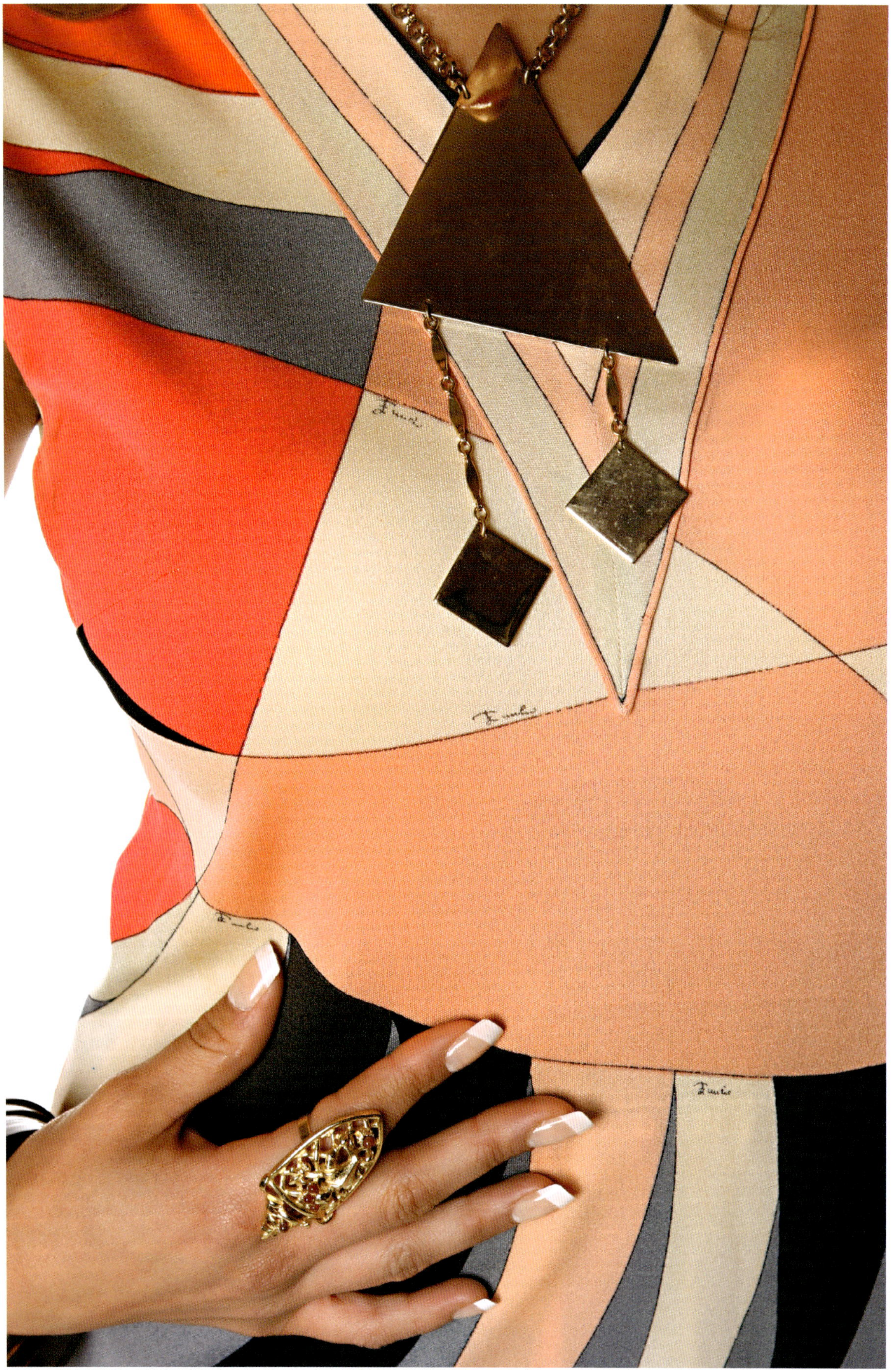

Opposite page: Somewhat of a dichotomy between the pale colors and the stark colors, the abstract print in this Pucci two-piece ensemble creates a movement that unifies the entire look. The black skin-tight boots have no label. The mirrored Lucite bangle bracelets and gypsy coin earrings are unmarked.

Close-up of Emilio signatures. This asymmetrical geometric necklace was designed by Bill De Seta for Accessocraft. The shield-shaped goldtone ring is unmarked.

Concentric circles of white enamel and gold plate formed a Space Age necklace with bravado. Massive links of white enamel and gold plate add the finishing touches to the overall scheme of things.

Close-up of the Emilio signature.

Pucci palazzo pajamas of a printed silk jersey top and a solid jade green harem style skirt. *Vogue*, May, 1964

Skirt and tunic top with Balinese print advertised in *Ladies' Home Journal*, July-August, 1963.

Pucci silk jersey dress and two-piece fringed outfit, both with similar prints in different color combinations, as seen in *Domenica del Corriere*, 1971.

Opposite page:
A casual look was achieved with this two-piece cotton outfit signed Emilio. The outfit is labeled Emilio Pucci, Florence, Italy. A separate store label reads: Exclusively for Saks Fifth Avenue. The loose-fitting silhouette of this ensemble created daytime drama. The craze for everything Pucci in the sixties created impetus for major department stores like Saks Fifth Avenue in New York City to open Pucci boutiques in all of their metropolitan locations. Major department stores across the country followed suit.

Opposite page:
The profusion of curvilinear lines, floral motifs and sinuous curves was the essence of the Art Nouveau style that Emilio Pucci succeeded in achieving when he masterfully created this print which was used for designing this extraordinary velvet evening gown. The exceptional choice of color compliments the print even further. This particular print was also available in other unique color schemes, as were many of Emilio Pucci's creations. As early as 1960, Liberty of London revived its original Art Nouveau prints, in particular its lotus prints. The original 1890s block prints were re-colored and made into exceptional silk fabric that Fontana of Rome used for designing dresses. This was the beginning of the renewal of the Art Nouveau revival in the sixties. Emilio Pucci was also instrumental in reviving the style and keeping it popular throughout the decade. As he set the pace throughout the sixties, a legion of copycat designers followed suit. By 1967, Art Nouveau prints in textile design really exploded in the fashion world. The original movement which began in the 1890s as a decorative style was characterized by curved lines, sinuous vines, abstract linear floral designs and flowing hair. Designers and artists like William Morris, Alphonse Mucha and Aubrey Beardsley set the tone for the original aesthetic movement which lasted about fifteen years.

Wide bangle bracelet made of glittery Lucite by unknown maker. Textured goldtone and faux emerald rhinestone drop earrings signed Bellini.

Rare men's Pucci blazer made of cotton velvet with unusual abstract print. The blazer is labeled Emilio Pucci by Ermenegildo Zegna, Tailored in Italy.

Take a closer look at the back of this blazer. How many Emilio signatures can you find?

Opposite page:
Pucci velvet dress with Empire waist, plunging neckline and banded borders. The engineered print establishes one look on the front and a completely different look on the back. The banding defines each area of the dress. Black suede sling-back heels by Via Spiga, Made in Italy.

Oversized girandole-style necklace composed of clear and black rhinestones in assorted shapes and sizes creating a spectacular neckpiece. Unfortunately, there are no maker's marks on this piece.

Close-up of two Emilio signatures found at the center of this abstract floral print which is exploding with color.

Close-up of Emilio signature and Mimi di N beaded necklace.

Side view of Dior suede and leather pumps with four inch heels.

Pucci created a perfect union between lightweight fabrics and heavyweight fabrics as seen here in the combination of a sheer printed silk blouse with heavy cotton velvet pants. It was a match made in heaven and Pucci designed these ensembles quite frequently. Beaded multi-strand necklace and earring set with faux pearl and rhinestone accents by Mimi di N.

To design is to plan and to organize, to order, to relate and to control. In short in embraces all means opposing disorder and accident. Therefore it signifies a human need and qualifies man's thinking and doing.
Josef Albers, in *Despite Straight Lines*, Yale University Press, 1961. **American Fabrics**, Spring 1965

Close-up of the Emilio signatures on the velvet geometric print jacket. Bib necklace made of turquoise glass beads accented with gold fluted beads creating a lattice effect. Ring made with a faux turquoise stone encased in a free form gold-plated setting, unmarked.

Front and back view of velvet cropped jacket and matching maxi skirt with an extraordinary geometric print closely resembling Pucci's Vivara print. Vivara was Emilio Pucci's first fragrance which was introduced in 1965. The vivid Mediterranean colors and perfectly executed print on this ensemble is the epitome of all that is Pucci.

Besides silk jersey being so comfortable to wear, it was easy to care for and a breeze to pack and travel with. A dozen or more Pucci silk jersey dresses or ensembles could easily fit into one suitcase. A perfect jet setters wardrobe!

Pucci two-piece ensemble designed with v-neck tunic top and matching palazzo pants made of featherweight silk jersey. Pucci two-piece suit lined with colorful signature fabric labeled Emilio Pucci by Ermenegildo Zegna, Tailored in Italy, Saks Fifth Avenue. Printed silk tie signed Emilio and labeled Emilio Pucci, Florence, Italy. Large Asian-inspired enameled pendant necklace, unmarked.

The same Pucci tunic top featured above and on the right, this time worn as a mini dress. Shoes by Charles Jourdan, Paris.

Left:
Pucci silk jersey midi dress with Empire waist, plunging neckline and full skirt. The exceptional peacock print is rendered in shades of pink on a black background. Pink peau de soie sling backs accented with clear rhinestones by Charles Jourdan, Paris. Pale pink Lucite fringed necklace by Tatiana, Made in Italy; earrings by Bellini.

Below:
The design of this dress and the fluidity of the fabric creates the perfect dress for a night on the town. Flamenco anyone?

Advertised for sale at Saks Fifth Avenue in the summer of 1966 as a slit skirt of jersey swirls of blue, green and black, the design is unmistakably Emilio Pucci and the fabric was made by Mabu. *Vogue*, June, 1966

Emilio Pucci silk jersey Empire waist dress with back slit over a leotard of the same sumptuous green and grape print. The outfit was advertised for sale at Neiman-Marcus and Saks Fifth Avenue. *Vogue*, June, 1966

Five colorful Pucci silk ties with wonderful prints.

Close-up of a few of the Emilio signatures found on the neckties.

Two-piece Pucci swimsuit made of printed Lycra. Printed beach towel made of cotton and labeled Emilio Pucci for Springmaid. Lucite sunglasses enhanced with clear rhinestones.

Springs Mills introduced it's striking new line of Emilio Pucci towels in a striking ballet by the Alwin Nikolais dancers at the George Abbott Theatre in New York. The Pucci towels are the first towels made by Spring Mills and feature the startling geometric designs and colors already made famous by Pucci in his "jet age" women's fashions. **American Fabrics**, Spring, 1967

Close-up of the Emilio signature on the Lycra swimsuit.

This engineered print designed by Emilio Pucci creates a unique look on the front as well as the back of this Lycra swimsuit. This was one of the many wonderful features of Pucci apparel that appealed to women all over the world. Within the same range of colors, Pucci created two distinct looks on the same garment. Deep purple metallic leather mules by Maud Frizon, Paris.

Close-up of the Emilio signature on the cotton swimsuit.

Dacron sail designed by Emilio Pucci for the AMF Alcott Sunfish as seen in *Vogue*, January, 1971. By the early 1970s, you can see how diverse the designs of Emilio Pucci were becoming.

Opposite page:
Front and back view of Pucci two-piece cotton swimsuit with a geometric print. The cut of this suit is very figure flattering. Purple metallic leather mules designed by Maud Frizon, Paris.

Emilio Pucci for Formfit Rogers—EPFR

In the late 1950s, Emilio Pucci teamed up with the Chicago foundations firm *Formfit-Rogers*. Pucci designed lingerie for women that accentuated their natural curves. His "natural girdle" in particular was designed in such a way as not to leave panty lines. This was so important for those women wearing his "Capri" pants and silk jersey tube dresses. Since the Pucci prints became in international success with high society and jet-setters, the need for these undergarments became a necessity. The stiff bras and girdles of the previous era were not appropriate for the silky fabrics that Pucci used. He designed slips, nightgowns, robes, bras, girdles, bed jackets, and even tights with wonderful prints. These garments were signed withthe initials EPFR (Emilio Pucci for Formfit-Rogers).

Nylon slip, bra and girdle with Art Nouveau print rendered in psychedelic colors signed EPFR.

Close-up of the EPFR signature on this "natural girdle" that Pucci designed to reveal the natural contours of the female body and not hide them.

LEONARD OF PARIS

Opposing page:
Luxurious silk jersey shirtwaist dress belted into shape with self-tied belt. The dress has short bell sleeves and banded borders. The oversized hydrangea print was executed in psychedelic colors. The dress is labeled Leonard of Paris for Bergdorf-Goodman and the Leonard signature is found many times in the print. Sling-back glitter pumps by Socialites.

Closer view of three Leonard signatures found in the print.

The genius behind the LEONARD label is Daniel Tribouillard. In the early fifties, Daniel Tribouillard began working at the French firm of Jacques Leonard. By 1958, Tribouillard was named Managing Artistic Director of Leonard Fashions. More than just a fashion designer, Daniel Tribouillard was an artist who created works of art on silken canvases. He favored exotic blossoms, especially orchids.

In 1960, Tribouillard invented a process of printing knitted fabrics, and by the early seventies, printed silk jersey dresses signed LEONARD were all the rage with the elite in Europe as well as the Unites States. The Leonard boutique opened in Paris in 1970. Tribouillard was often referred to as the "French Pucci" In 1974, the price of a matte silk dress accompanied by a matching fringed shawl and printed with his famous orchid pattern retailed for $550.00, a hefty sum to pay at that time. Leonard Fashions were sold in major department stores and specialty boutiques. Today there are over 120 Leonard boutiques worldwide.

Printed gown by LEONARD Fashion for Bergdorf Goodman, advertised in *Vogue*, March, 1972.

Asian-inspired tunic top and matching pants by LEONARD Fashion, Paris, for Bergdorf Goodman on the Plaza, New York. *Vogue,* November, 1972

Silk jersey gown with matching turban by LEONARD Fashion, Paris, for Bergdorf Goodman, as advertised in *Vogue*, September, 1973.

Leopard print silk jersey dress and matching leopard safari hat by LEONARD Fashion, Paris, for Bergdorf Goodman on the Plaza, New York. *Vogue*, September, 1974

LILLY PULITZER

A Lilly Pulitzer maxi dress with a captivating tulip print rendered in vibrant neon colors. The dress was designed with a fitted waist, full skirt, ruffles around the collar and hemline and rick rack trim. The dress is labeled The Lilly, Lilly Pulitzer, and signed Lilly throughout the print. Abstract printed turban, no label. Royal blue peep toe sling backs by Claudio Rocco, Made in Italy.

Oversized Maltese cross pendant necklace set with large faux gemstones and enamel ornamentation by Castlecliff.

Mod ball drop earrings enameled and swirled in gold, unmarked.

Close-up of Lilly signature hidden in the print. Sometimes Lilly signatures are a little hard to find; this one kind of blends in with the print.

Lillian Lee McKim, later known as Lilly Pulitzer, was born in Roslyn, New York, in the 1930s. She eloped with Herbert (Peter) Pulitzer and moved to Palm Beach, Florida, where they raised three children. Peter was involved with his many citrus groves and Lilly, a bored and wealthy housewife, wanted something to do. She decided to open a juice stand in a fancy neighborhood of Palm Beach. Her little business became quite a hit, but day after day, squeezing oranges, lemons, and limes made stains on her clothing. She asked her dressmaker to design her some sort of uniform to wear to work at her fruit stand that would somehow hide all the stains. Out of cheap, printed cotton fabric from a local five-and-ten cents store, the "Lilly" dress was born.

In no time, Lilly Pulitzer's cute little cotton shifts were selling to Palm Beach women faster than her juice drinks. She decided to stop selling the juice and pursue a career designing and selling her dresses. She used colorful printed cotton fabrics, lined her dresses and cleverly signed them with the name *Lilly* hidden in the print. When her long time friend Jacqueline Bouvier, then Jackie Kennedy, was pictured in *Life Magazine* wearing one of her dresses, The Lilly became a huge success. The line became more elaborate season after season incorporating hostess gowns, maxi dresses, culottes, shorts, skirts and palazzo pants. Lilly Pulitzer Boutiques opened up in resort areas across the country and Lilly's clothing was quickly adopted by jet setters. Popularity increased throughout the late sixties and by the early seventies, Lilly Pulitzer Men's Stuff line was introduced. Children's apparel was also marketed. In 1984, Lilly closed her business due to bankruptcy only to reopen with more interest than ever in 1993. The line is extremely popular today.

Close-up of the Lilly signature found in the print. Oversized jewel encrusted ball drop pendant necklace by Schreiner. A closer view of the cobalt blue glass multi-strand bracelet by DeMario shows round and smooth beads, faceted beads and flat beads.

Hostess gown by Lilly Pulitzer made of a heavy acrylic fabric printed with large blooms and leaves rendered in shades of blue, green and gold. Model is also wearing DeMario glass earrings and matching bracelet. The gold leather slippers by Oomphies were made in Spain.

Close-up of Lilly signature strategically placed in the print. This signature was really hard to find!

A pretty pastel floral print was used to create this peek-a-boo pants and top outfit labeled The Lilly, Palm Beach, Florida. The fabric is also signed Lilly. Sherbert green plastic bangle bracelet and dome earrings studded with brass by Accessocraft. Mod style glittered Lucite dome ring, unmarked. The pastel beaded barrel-shaped handbag is labeled B.B., Made in Hong Kong. Shoes by Nina, Made in Spain.

Spring and summer Lilly Pulitzer fashions, as advertised in *Harper's Bazaar*, March and June of 1971.

Men's printed blazer and a woman's summer shift by Lilly Pulitzer, as advertised in *Harper's Bazaar* in July of 1971.

Men's printed slacks and a woman's coordinated outfit by Lilly Pulitzer, as advertised in *Vogue* in January of 1972.

Spring and fall Lilly Pulitzer fashions, as advertised in *Vogue*, April and November of 1970.

> *If textile prints present an astonishing panorama of inventiveness, beauty and color, it must in great measure be attributed to the inspiration of floral forms.*
> **American Fabrics,** Fall-Winter, 1963

Closer view of the Marc signature found in the print. Notice how the orange beads have a moonglow look to them.

Cleverly designed hostess or lounging gown with webbed batwing sleeves, Empire waist and allover abstract floral print signed Marc. The fabric is a billowy polyester. This type of garment, designed for at-home wear, was also called a caftan. They were very popular in the sixties and seventies and the perfect wardrobe choice for entertaining at home. The double strand of bright orange Lucite beads is unmarked. Orange Lucite and metal tambourine bangle bracelet, also unmarked.

MAURICE

Opposite page:
Cascading hand-manipulated bib neckpiece composed of clear faceted crystals, smooth amber glass beads and rhinestone rondelles. Although this piece is unmarked, it could possibly be the work of Mimi di N. Glitzy rhinestone drop earrings by Mimi di N. Oversized amber glass cameo and filigree cuff bracelet, unmarked.

Close-up of Maurice signature and the turquoise leather mules by Kimel.

Eastern influenced silk jersey gown with Empire waist signed Maurice. This gown is labeled Peck & Peck, Fifth Avenue, New York. Again we see banding around the scoop neckline, Empire waist and hemline, and an intricate print, which creates a look similar to Emilio Pucci, Bessi and Leonard of Paris. Quite obviously influenced by those designers, Maurice signature prints were also sold in fine department stores. Prices varied depending on the fabric used and the complexity of the prints. The appeal of jersey knit, whether it was made of silk or even nylon, was synonymous with comfort as well as easy care and a perfect choice for travel. The signature prints were extremely popular with the jet set and their popularity was spilling out into the volume market. The signature provided a status symbol and throughout the sixties and early seventies, these prints were everywhere.

An exceptionally large gold-plated pendant designed with heavy embossing and enhanced with a large faux amethyst surrounded by faux pearls also doubles as a brooch. The lovely bracelet and earring demi-parure made of fancy gold-plated metal and square-cut amethyst glass stones, is unmarked.

Black nylon jersey maxi dress with floral print, fitted waist and banded borders. The dress is labeled and signed Maurice. Black strappy sandals by Jolene.

Close-up of the Maurice signature cleverly positioned on the leaf.

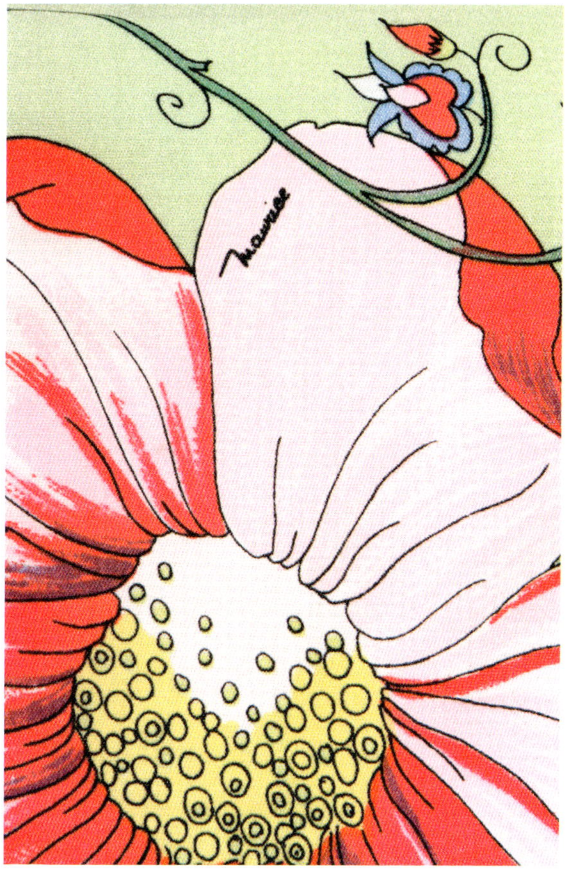

Close-up of the Maurice signature on the flower petal.

Pale green was the perfect backdrop for the pretty flower garden rendered in shades of pink, red, yellow and dark green. The clever positioning of the banding creates an angular neckline. It also accentuates the waist, sleeves and hemline. Striking necklace with faux emerald beaded chain by Lucien Piccard. Emerald green enameled bangle bracelet by Boucher.

Emerald green crocheted cap covered with the same color spangles or pailettes. Atomic style pin and earring demi-parure made with green cascading plastic tendrils. Oversized emerald green confetti Lucite bangle bracelet by unknown maker.

A dichromatic print on a long sleeve shift dress has been loosely belted with a self-tied belt. The dress is signed and labeled Maurice. Dark green patent leather t-straps by Hi-Brows.

A closer view of the atomic-style demi-parure shows how the pin and earrings hang like a fireworks display. Ring made with a molded green plastic rosebud perched on a free form gold-plated setting with rhinestone accents.

Like all pioneers, Count Pucci – who created a revolution seasons back – would be amazed at the expanding markets opened up by his original printed silk jersey…to say nothing of his silk stretch pants, bathing suits, evening dresses, blouses and sportswear – all packable for travel.
American Fabrics, Winter, 1961-62

Long sleeve button-down day dress made of nylon jersey with a psychedelic mushroom print. The dress is signed Maurice and labeled Maurice by C.Rizza. Enid Collins canvas and jeweled handbag called "Castaway" and signed Collins. Lizard grained leather and clear Lucite sling-back pumps by J.Renee.

Check out the Maurice signature cleverly perched on the cap of the mushroom.

Choker necklace made of large rectangular-cut and faceted salmon-colored gemstones, unmarked. Cluster earrings and orange Lucite dome ring, also unmarked. Closer view of the Collins jeweled handbag.

Two-piece ensemble consisting of a sleeveless gown designed with a scoop neckline, Empire waist and matching jacket labeled and signed Maurice. The abstract random print is rendered in a profusion of lively colors which compliment the overall design. Influenced by Emilio Pucci, clothing designed by C.Rizza for Maurice can also be termed "Pucci-esque". Sometimes the term "pseudo-Pucci" is even used to describe these wonderful signature prints. Although this outfit was made of nylon stretch knit and came with a lower price tag than a real Pucci, the overall print appeal was still very eye-catching.

Silver metallic open toe sling-backs with a classic seventies lattice design by Fantura. Close-up of the Maurice signature displayed in a very obvious location on the print.

Bottom right:
Necklace and earring set made of silver-plated metal with pastel pink drops by Napier. Hexagon-shaped Lucite bangle bracelet made to look like mother of pearl and enhanced with silver glitter inserts.

MR. DINO

Spectacular maxi skirt and fringed shawl ensemble made of nylon jersey with a dramatic Op Art print executed in shades of yellow on a black background. Signed and labeled Mr. Dino, this outfit was cutting edge in the sixties. Choker necklace of twisted black silk cord accented with large fluted beads of gold-plated metal. Canary yellow ankle strap heels by Captivators.

Op Art is an influential source of textile design and will unquestionably expand in the coming seasons.
American Fabrics, Spring, 1965

Mr. Dino created fashion drama in the front as well as the back of this artistic print which is overflowing with boldness, dimension and bravado. He sure didn't hide the signature in this print!

The same version of the powerful Mr. Dino Op Art print as seen in the previous two pages but this time in shades of Mediterranean blue on a black background and made into a long velvet maxi skirt. Inspiration for Op Art in textile design was drawn from the international art exhibit of 125 paintings titled the "Responsive Eye" which was held in New York's Museum of Modern Art in 1965. Fashion and fabric designers utilized these art techniques applying them to textile design. Clothing has often been described as "wearable art" during this period.

Glamorous necklace and matching earrings set with rhinestones in assorted sizes, shapes and colors. The set is unfortunately unmarked. Juliana style large link bracelet made with oversized emerald-cut faux sapphire stones.

Simple designs which attract and hold attention are obviously of interest to the fabric and fashion industries, and it is on this level that Op Art scores most heavily. The practitioners – and "practitioners" describes their scientific coolly unemotional approach – of Op Art use such basic elements as squares, circles, spirals, and the like to build designs which frequently offer multiple interpretations. Many of the principles employed are those of the "optical illusions" familiar to all of us – cubes which alternately advance and recede, spirals of brilliant color which seem to rotate, complex patterns of large dots which mesmerize the beholder.
American Fabrics, Spring, 1965

Art Deco style geometric pendant necklace with cream and black enamel signed Castlecliff. Octagon-shaped Lucite ring set in gold-plated metal, unmarked.

Mr. Dino used the same Op Art print in a different color combination to create another stunning two-piece outfit, this time with a shorter skirt and a long sleeve top with a peplum reminiscent of the 1940s. Tan and black leather t-strap shoes by Gucci, Made in Italy.

When Emilio Pucci created his silk jersey dresses with his wonderful signed prints, many other designers and manufacturers were inspired by his work. Some set out to make copies made of inexpensive fabrics while others had a unique style all of their own. During the late fifties, in a small warehouse in Miami, Florida, a man by the name of Max Cohen created fabulous prints that were signed *Mr. Dino.* Since his wife was a big fan of Dean Martin, the name *Mr. Dino* was the brain child of Mrs. Cohen and it turned out to be the right name for the business.

All throughout the sixties, fashion consumers had a huge appetite for prints. Beginning early in the decade with Art Nouveau prints and running the gamut of Art Deco, Pop Art, Flower Power, Persian, Baroque, abstracts and geometrics, Mr. Dino satisfied the needs of the volume market with his wonderful silk screened signature prints. He also used a range of fabrics from Avril rayon, Arnel, Celanese, Fortrel, cotton, velvet, nylon jersey and others designed for comfort, durability, easy in laundering and of course packability for travel. Fashions by Mr. Dino were sold in major department stores like I.Magnin, Bergdorf Goodman, Sakowitz, Marshall Field, Filenes and Lord & Taylor. Many consider Mr. Dino to have been a rival to Emilio Pucci.

Maxi skirt made of nylon jersey with another of Mr. Dino's famous Op Art prints. This print was artistically rendered in shades of pink on a black background. The print is signed Mr. Dino. A long black silk chiffon and gold glitter rectangular scarf was made into a halter top. Mod earrings made of hot pink sequins. Swiss made mod watch with a wide hot pink vinyl band by Miss London.

Close-up of the Mr. Dino signature followed by the copyright symbol.

Close-up of the Miss London hot pink vinyl watch.

The same skirt on a different model worn with a different top creating a totally different look. The captivating Op Art print is on the back of the skirt as well.

The tendency to engineer prints specifically for use in shifts is taking on more strongly than many people realize. The bold, colorful print patterns are designed to necessitate a minimum of cutting and sewing. The designers are finding them lots of fun, too, since the sky is practically the limit as far as ideas and execution are concerned.
American Fabrics, Winter, 1964-65

This signature was found in a very unusual place right at the hemline. Occasionally I have seen Mr. Dino signatures right on the hem on the inside of the dress in some very obscure locations. Most of the time, however, the signatures are very visible.

Long sleeve shift dress made of double knit polyester with another fabulous Mr. Dino Op Art print. This one is signed Mr. Dino Inc. with the copyright symbol. Beaded open toe sling-backs made of silk by Bruno Magli.

Close-up of the Art Deco style pendant necklace made of black Lucite with gold-plated trim and chain by Trifari.

Another variation of the Mr. Dino Op Art print made into a polyester chemise. Black Lucite bangle bracelet enhanced with clear rhinestones by Accessocraft. Enamel dome ring, unmarked. Art Deco style pendant necklace made of Lucite with gold-plated accents by Trifari. Huge rhinestone clip earrings by Juliana (DeLizza & Elster). Two-toned spectator style pumps by Morgan Taylor.

Closer view of the Mr. Dino signature in the print accompanied by the copyright symbol. Many of the popular Mr. Dino prints were copyrighted, along with many of the prints designed by Gene Berk for Paganne.

Op Art (short for Optical) and Pop Art have more in common than their short, catchy, rhyming names. For one thing, they share a deliberate attempt to bemuse the mind as well as delight the eye. Also, both Op and Pop rject the free painterly qualities of action painting in favor of tightly organized flat areas of solid color.
American Fabrics, Spring, 1965

Printed polyester knit tunic top from the early sixties labeled Mr. Dino, New York, Paris, Florence. Chandelier-style earrings made of filigree and clear crystals. Pair of square mirrored Lucite bracelets by Accessocraft.

Mr. Dino hand-printed and signed double knit Fortrel polyester top and matching wide-legged pants with a solid black sash. *Vogue*, December, 1968

Advertised as "piquant and petalled", this Mr. Dino midi-dress with handkerchief style hem was made of Arnel triacetate. It was sold at Bergdorf Goodman on the Plaza in New York, I.Magnin, West Coast, Burdines's, Miami and Marshall Field in Chicago. *Vogue*, January, 1971

Mr. Dino fashions from 1967 made of Celanese Arnel triacetate which was manufactured into a textured double knit and advertised as a washable, comfortable, wrinkle resistant and packable.

Evening gown designed with fitted waist, stand-up collar and matching fringed shawl. The captivating print was executed in Caribbean colors. Notice how the banding echoes the print on a smaller scale. This wonderful ensemble is signed and labeled Mr. Dino.

Fabulous hand-manipulated three-dimensional neckpiece made of turquoise glass drops, faceted aurora borealis crystals and gold-plated coral-shaped beads. Possibly another Mimi di N masterpiece. Turquoise and milk glass cluster earrings, unknown maker.

Close-up of the Mr. Dino signature. Gold metallic pumps accented with glittery inserts by Imperial.

The screen method of printing textiles, though more expensive than roller printing, has significant advantages. From the point of view of design, pattern repeats can be much larger and since the process is slower, pigment colors can be laid on in heavy layers to produce handicraft effects.
American Fabrics, Fall-Winter, 1963

The sixties was a wonderful decade filled with grandeur in many forms and costume jewelry was at the top of the list. Many pendants, bracelets, earrings, rings and huge bib necklaces were oversized and the appeal was overwhelming. The jewelry looked sensational with the prints of the same era. This oversized cross pendant necklace made of large white cabochons accented with clear rhinestones and set in japanned metal is marked Schreiner, New York. Black enameled openwork earrings styled by Accessocraft. Black and white bangle bracelet with hand painted geometrics, unmarked.

Close-up of the Mr. Dino© signature with the copyright symbol.

Tunic top with black and white Art Nouveau style print signed Mr. Dino. This type of Art Nouveau print was most likely inspired by the linear black and white renderings of Aubrey Beardsley, who was a leader in the original movement which began at the end of the 19th century. The black and white plastic bangle bracelet is unmarked. Black patent leather pumps by Imperial.

One of the major influences not to be overlooked in the simplicity of the fashion silhouette. Shifts, straight-toppers, sheaths have made possible – indeed – demand – boldness of fabric design. **American Fabrics**, Summer, 1966

Rhodium-plated coiled mesh snake bracelet with jeweled eyes by Whiting & Davis. Stylized floral drop earrings set with black rhinestones and accented with a faux pearl signed Bellini.

Sleeveless double knit shift designed with a Peter Pan collar and Art Nouveau style print signed and labeled Mr. Dino. A rhodium-plated mesh snake belt gently hangs at the waist. Royal blue grosgrain peep toe sling backs by Claudio Rocco.

Close-up of the Mr. Dino© signature cleverly positioned in the Art Nouveau print. Again we see the copyright symbol which is found on many Mr. Dino garments.

Right:
Close-up of the Mr. Dino signature positioned near the bottom of the dress. Again, a copyright symbol is visible. Copyright symbols followed the Mr. Dino signature whereas they preceded the Paganne signatures.

Left:
Button-down long sleeve shift made of Fortrel polyester with an abstract print signed Mr. Dino. Gold metallic leather mules by Peppers made in Italy. Textured gold-plated dome ring by Vendome. Oversized white straw handbag by Marcus Brothers of Miami.

Below:
Enchanting demi-parure consisting of a choker necklace and matching clip earrings set with large and unusual emerald-cut stones accented with aurora borealis rhinestones. The set was made by Florenza. Large faux pearls were coated with three different metallic colors forming an adorable bauble bracelet by an unknown maker.

Fabrics that stretch were not discovered yesterday. They have a long history. The elegant hose of Shakespeare's' Hamlet...the seductive costumes of Degas' ballet dancers...the constricting girdles of the 20th century American women...these and many, many other garments have long been made of fabrics which stretch. And it is an obvious truth that all knitted fabrics, in one sense are stretchable, as against most woven fabrics that are rigid.
American Fabrics, Winter-Spring, 1964

Red, white and blue printed maxi skirt with matching cropped jacket made of stretch knit and signed Mr. Dino. The red, white and blue canvas espadrilles were made in Spain. White plastic cube charm bracelet, maker unknown.

The same Mr. Dino two-piece ensemble worn a little more daring. Thin strips of blue and white plastic were used to design these mod earrings by Paco Rabanne. The bright red ring was made of Bakelite.

For a society which is as mobile as ours, which lives in cars and planes and travels light over the wide surface of the globe, the modern breed of knits answers the need of the times. "Have knits...will travel" would be an apt slogan for the day. They pack easily and in little space, they hang out free of wrinkles, they are comfortable to wear, easy to care for and wearable with elegance for any and all occasions.
American Fabrics, Winter, 1965-66

One-piece knit jumpsuit with Middle Eastern print rendered in psychedelic colors and signed Mr. Dino. Peep toe platform shoes in silver and blue metallic leather by Albert Durelle. Pink and blue plastic bangle bracelets enhanced with brass studs styled by Accessocraft; large pink plastic hoop earrings to match.

Knit sheath dress made of polyester with a rainbow print bodice and cuffs signed Mr. Dino. Silk pumps with rainbow print by Life Stride.

Closer view of the Mr. Dino© signature. Mod ring made of layers of multi-colored Lucite adding to the rainbow theme.

POP PRINTS – A New Dramatic Art Form Puts Fun Into Apparel Fabric Design!
American Fabrics, Winter, 1964-65

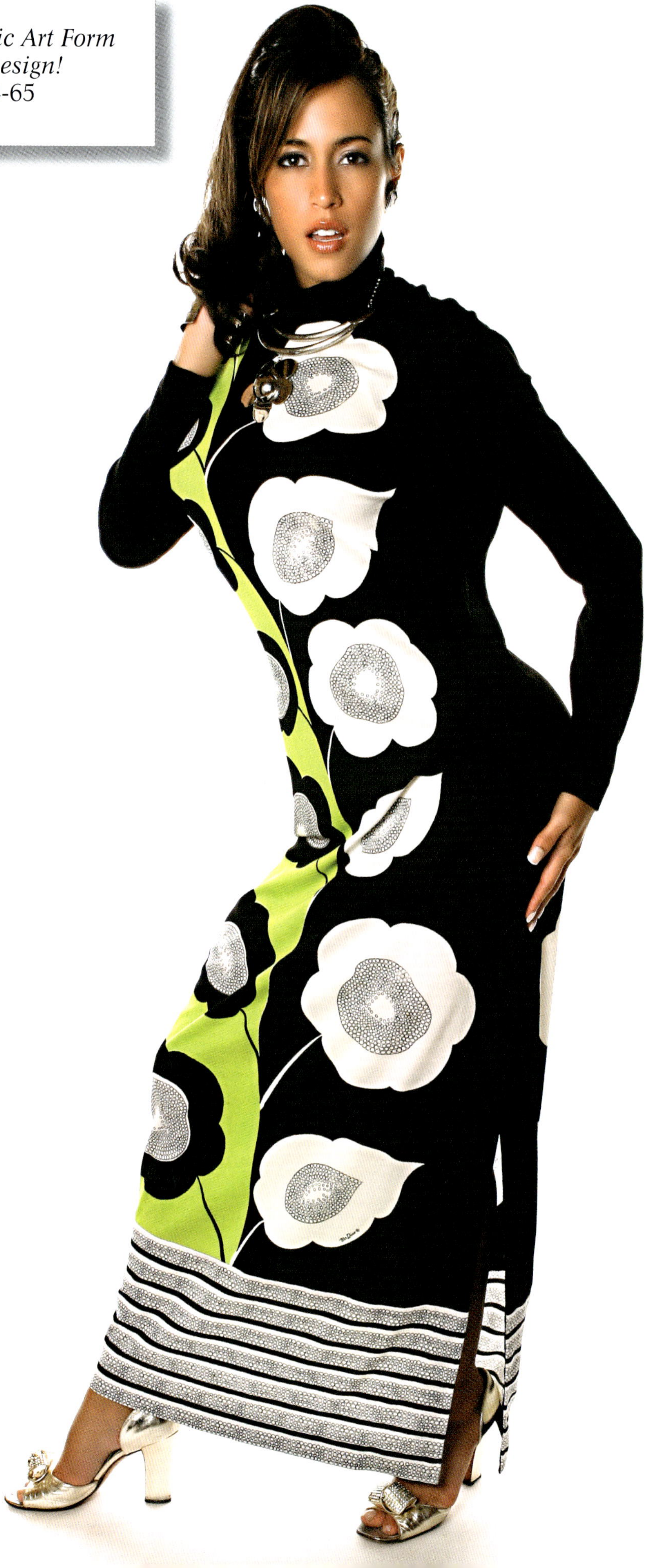

The choker necklace made of silvertone metal with a huge floral centerpiece screams flower power. Wide cuff bracelet made of sterling silver stamped Italy. The shell clip earrings are unmarked.

Close-up of the Mr. Dino signature accompanied by the copyright symbol. Silver metallic leather and jeweled open-toe pumps by Ravne, Ltd., Shoemakers to Her Majesty the Queen.

Opposite page:
Long sheath dress made of nylon jersey designed with a stand-up collar and side slit. The oversized print and color scheme was derived from the artistic movement, Pop Art, that dominated the fashion scene in the mid-sixties. Sources of inspiration for the sixties textile designer came from artists like Robert Indiana and Jasper Johns. In this instance, a basic flower and leaf print was transformed into a stunning gown by use of color and the principles of design.

Fancy fluted ball and chain necklace made of gold-plated metal by an unknown maker. Clip earrings with goldtone drops, unmarked.

A design technique called Trompe-l'oeil was cleverly used here when designing this dress which actually looks like a cropped jacket over a straight shift. The dress is signed and labeled Mr. Dino. Lucite and gold mules by Frederick's of Hollywood.

Here we have a closer view of the atomic style demi-parure which looks like a fireworks display.

The stained glass print has a richness which derives from clarity and precision in printing. It combines both a medieval and contemporary feeling with compelling effect.
American Fabrics, Spring, 1963

Long sleeve maxi dress designed with an Empire waist, stand-up collar and front slit. The exceptional stained glass print was rendered in a kaleidoscope of psychedelic colors and executed on nylon jersey. The banded borders accentuate the overall design. Pink peau de soie peep toe sling backs with rhinestone ornamentation by Charles Jourdan, Paris. Deep purple plastic atomic style brooch and earring set, unmarked.

When Pucci started it all a decade ago, the taste for chiffon-weight knits began steadily to increase. Having once savored the sensuous comfort of these fluid Pucci-type dresses, women will not easily give them up.
American Fabrics, Winter, 1965-66

Talk about the power of the flower print: this sleeveless tunic with matching maxi skirt gets belted into shape to form a striking silhouette signed Mr. Dino. Often referred to as a watercolor print, the intricacy of the print, the pastel colors used on the black background and the long lean look was cutting edge fashion drama in the sixties. Lucite and gold mules by Frederick's of Hollywood.

Asian-inspired medallion made of simulated jade by unknown maker. Bauble bracelet made of assorted beads in different shades of green. Three-dimensional goldtone clip earrings with floral motifs, also unmarked.

A close-up of the Mr. Dino© signature discreetly positioned in the print and the Lucite mules by Frederick's of Hollywood.

Striking evening gown made of nylon jersey with a exotic Persian print executed in vibrant colors. The dress is signed Mr. Dino and labeled Mr. Dino, New York, Paris, Florence. Black suede pumps by Via Spiga, Made in Italy.

Wide hinged cuff bracelet made of Russian gold-plate with elaborate embossed designs is signed Miriam Haskell. Intricate gold-plated necklace and drop earring set accented with mother of pearl tusks and faux rubies. This set is unmarked but looks almost identical to one made by Kenneth J. Lane. Figural ring set with faux coral and turquoise stones, unmarked.

In a shrinking world, with jet planes bringing far-off places almost into our backyard, designers have unlimited scope for source inspiration.
American Fabrics, Fall-Winter ,1963

Spectacular multi-colored Lucite neckpiece and matching dangle earrings designed with a unique combination of large faceted beads and smooth plastic discs creating a three-dimensional effect. This is possibly the work of Mimi di N but it is unfortunately unmarked. Enameled dome ring in sea foam green with faux coral stones, unmarked.

Close-up of the Mr. Dino signature hidden in the floral print.

The world is not bored with prints. If fashion is one of the chief ways for a woman to express her individuality, prints give her one of the chief means to do that. And now that patterns are crossing international borders as quickly as the jet stream, a woman can express her individuality in many languages. Vive le print!
American Fabrics, Spring, 1968

Body hugging chemise with an exciting floral print rendered in eye-popping exotic colors. Creative banding at the neckline adds an Asian feel to the overall silhouette. The dress is made of nylon jersey and signed Mr. Dino with the accompanying copyright symbol found on so many of Mr. Dino prints. Gold metallic leather peep toe wedgies accented with jewels and sequins by Caparros.

Close-up of the Mr. Dino signature followed by the copyright symbol.

Closer view of the amulet necklace and the Baroque print.

Short sleeve tunic top with Baroque print made of polyester and signed Mr. Dino. Amulet style necklace of gold-plated metal and plastic beads made to look like gemstones in the rough. Chunky glass beaded bracelet and earring set reminiscent of the work of Miriam Haskell or Robert DeMario but unfortunately unmarked.

Long sleeve nylon jersey button-down blouse with another wonderful Baroque print signed Mr. Dino. Border designs in contrasting colors created a sophisticated look. Austrian crystal drop earrings by Bellini.

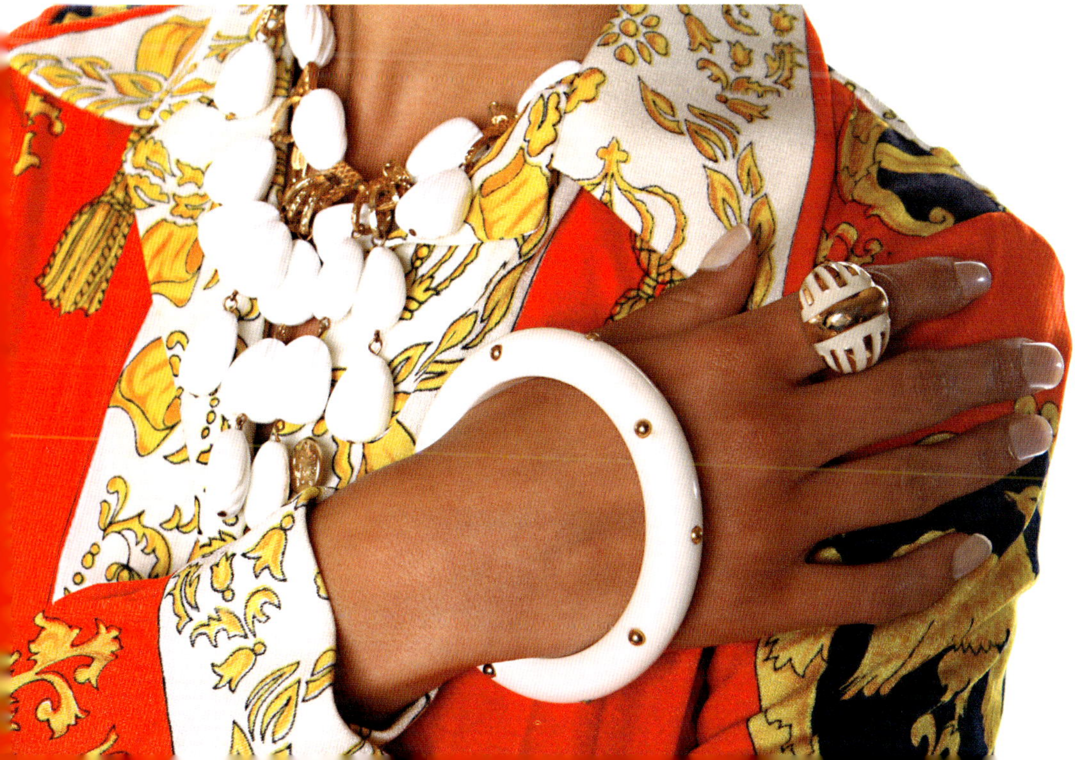

Fringed necklace made of gold-plated metal and cascading fluted white plastic beads, unmarked. White plastic bangle bracelet enhanced with brass studs by Accessocraft. Gold-plated and white enamel dome ring, unmarked.

It is true that there has been an almost insatiable desire for glitter and sparkle in fabrics.
American Fabrics, Summer, 1967

Bonded metallic knit party dress with an Art Nouveau print rendered in neon colors. The dress is signed Mr. Dino. Multi-colored metallic t-strap shoes by Pollini, Italy.

Huge neckpiece with double lion motif rendered in gold plate and further embellished with a large carnelian cabochon and smaller faux emerald drops.

Close-up of the Mr. Dino signature accompanied by the copyright symbol.

For the volume fashion market, the big niche for chiffon-weight knits is being filled by the man-made fibers rather than by the silks which Pucci originally used. Fine gauge chiffon-weight jerseys knitted of 100 percent Antron nylon are ideal for this favorite, especially in the deep, rich color prints to which the fabric lends itself. They meet a demand which remains undiminished since design and color play such an important part of this volume category. **American Fabrics,** Winter, 1965-66

Nylon jersey dress designed with a solid bodice and needlepoint print skirt accented with banded borders and silk fringed sleeves. The dress is signed Mr. Dino. The signature was actually found on the inside of the dress right on the hem. Yellow ankle strap leather pumps by Captivators. Oversized neckpiece of heavy gold-plated metal accented with black stones and drops marked SUL. The Lucite bangle bracelet with rhinestone accents was made by Accessocraft.

Nylon jersey maxi skirt with a tri-color daisy print signed Mr. Dino. Black and yellow polka dot bangle bracelet made of Lucite by Accessocraft. Plastic and wood necklace designed by Kenneth J. Lane. Bright yellow leather ankle strap pumps by Captivators.

Don't pity the humble daisy. It has captured the fancy of a whole group of imaginative textile designers. They have used it in large and small scale designs to create a flower look in fashion. The humblest of flowers has become one of the noblest designs. **American Fabrics**, Fall-Winter, 1967

Close-up of the Mr. Dino signature amidst the floral bouquet. A copyright symbol is also present.

Queenly Qiana makes an exclusive entrance. It has always been man's dream to reproduce silk by his own hand – and Qiana is the closest to that dream yet.
American Fabrics, Spring, 1969

Floral printed maxi skirt made of Qiana nylon and signed Mr. Dino. During the late sixties, simplicity in the actual silhouette was enhanced with the boldness and often complex fabric designs that were readily available. An otherwise simple maxi skirt, tunic, shift or sheath dress would come to life with the innovative prints of the day.

Fancy cut foil-backed aurora borealis crystal drop earrings, unmarked. The stones look strikingly similar to the modern day mystic topaz stones that are so popular now. Hot pink enameled openwork pendant necklace, also unmarked.

Tunic top made of nylon jersey with a Persian print rendered in psychedelic colors on a black background. The top is signed and labeled Mr. Dino. Wide banding of a contrasting color accentuates the cuffs and hemline while a smaller version of the same print is used as a Nehru-style collar.

OGUST

Catherine Ogust designed simple shirt-dresses for Penthouse Gallery in New York with bold prints, mandarin collars and knotted monkey fist buttons. Obi-style sashes also accompanied the dresses and when tied, the simple dress looked somewhat like a Japanese kimono. Sometimes the dresses were worn without the sash. Big, bold prints in two or three colors were popular as well as prints utilizing a rainbow of colors. This particular cotton shirtdress with a bold print was rendered in black, white and mocha. It is signed Ogust.

Rhinestone enhanced plastic eyeglasses by unknown maker. Paper thin plastic strips in black and white were used by designer Paco Rabanne to create these mod earrings. The long ball and chain necklace in black and gold is unmarked.

It is no contradiction to feature black-and-white in the midst of fashion's current color extravaganza. Fashion-wise buyers are complaining that black-and-white dresses are hard to find in the market and are much in demand by consumers. Alongside the continuing interest in bold color they note a strong and persistent demand for the stark and simplicity of black-and-white fashions.
American Fabrics, Summer, 1961

Cotton shirtdress with bold black and white abstract print, belted into shape with a corresponding sash. The print is signed Ogust and labeled Catherine Ogust for Penthouse Gallery. The black skin-tight boots have no label.

Geometric beads in black and white plastic reinforcing the positive and negative feel of this ensemble. Mod designer earrings by Paco Rabanne made of paper thin strips of black and white plastic. The black and white thermoplastic link bracelet is by an unknown manufacturer.

The same shirtdress on a different model, worn without the sash. A pair of heels was substituted instead of the boots creating a totally different look. Notice the mandarin collar and wide sash. When the sash is tied a certain way, the dress is reminiscent of a Japanese kimono.

Close-up of Ogust signature.

PAGANNE

Evening gown of Antron nylon with a dichromatic print made up of large blooms and geometric designs. The dress is signed ©Paganne and was popular in 1972. Triple-strand bracelet and cluster earring demi-parure made of clear and amber crystals accented with clear rhinestones by unknown maker. Art Deco style faux pearls and clear Lucite necklace. The Lucite was made to look like rock crystal which was very popular for jewelry manufacture in the 1920s.

Close-up of the Paganne signature accompanied by a copyright symbol.

Draped triple-strand necklace made of faux pearls, aurora borealis crystals and abstract goldtone beads. Link bracelet and drop earring set of red and white cabochons in gold-plated metal, maker unknown. The bracelet has a toggle closure. Notice the Paganne signature on the sleeve with the copyright symbol.

Gene Berk did not set out to be a fashion designer. Initially, he was a pre-law student who went on to merchandise menswear and finally worked with Oleg Cassini before going out on his own. By 1967, the 31-year old had an office on Madison Avenue in New York City and traveled back and forth across the Atlantic to Milan or Como, Italy where his eye-catching signature prints were skillfully made by experts in the field. His Paganne, Ltd. became a subsidiary of the Dress Division of Printogs, Ltd.

Gene Berk was another contemporary of Emilio Pucci who signed his prints and his clothing became a worldwide sensation with the jet setters traveling to resorts from one continent to the next. He used many fabrics including cottons, velvets, wool and synthetics but his prized prints were rendered on a very lightweight and desirable silk jersey.

Gene Berk was a master creating engineered prints which he then designed into the actual garment. Many of his popular prints were used for designing different forms of apparel.. For instance, the same print could be made into a long dinner dress as well as a pair of halter pajamas or a simple shift. Another engineered print was available in an evening dress as well as a day dress. He designed scenic prints, abstract prints and geometrics. He dabbled in trompe-l'oeil in addition to prints with Grecian, Egyptian and French motifs. Op Art and Pop Art were also well received. Paganne Ltd. fashions were sold in fine department stores in Europe and America. They are extremely desirable today and command high prices at auction.

Reports of the decline of the print have been widely exaggerated. It has merely become more sophisticated and internationalized – and lovelier on a larger scale.
American Fabrics, Spring, 1968

White parasol-shaped blossoms cascade down this bright red maxi dress made of nylon jersey and signed ©Paganne. The square neckline is further enhanced with ruffles. The dress is labeled Paganne Ltd. by Gene Berk. White leather heels accented with large buckles are labeled Bellini.

> *In this year of print explosion, boldness of design and brilliance of color dominate the print scene.*
> **American Fabrics,** Winter-Spring, 1967

Eight-strand plastic and metal draped necklace in an interesting green and purple color combination by Kramer. Link bracelet and large clip earring set made of embossed antiqued metal and faux amethyst stones. Unfortunately, this set bears no maker's marks.

Rhythm in motion describes this maxi dress with bold print executed in a vibrant color scheme. The Empire waist and side slit create a sexy silhouette. The dress is signed Paganne. This particular design, along with many of the other Paganne prints were rendered in different color schemes and made in different styles. This was common with Gene Berk designs. This particular print was not copyrighted as were most of his later designs. Deep purple metallic leather mules designed by Maud Frizon, Paris.

A Parisian mural on a nylon jersey canvas was designed by Gene Berk for Paganne. This print was also offered in different color schemes. Maxi dresses were available as well as the shorter version of this popular print. Spectator style pumps by Morgan Taylor, Spain. Jeweled canvas handbag with a French motif designed by Enid Collins. A perfect tote bag for carrying Kia!

Spectacular five-strand draped neckpiece with a center medallion of cascading French jet and gold glass beads. Unfortunately this piece is unmarked. Black filigree earrings and black hexagon-shaped Lucite bangle set with amber glass stones, both styled by Accessocraft.

Close-up of the ©Paganne signature.

Close-up of the ©Paganne signature.

A plunging neckline, banded borders and a bold color combination makes this dress signed Paganne real eye-catching. It's hard to be this dress is almost 40 years old! It looks very contemporary. Lucite and gold mules by Frederick's of Hollywood.

"Vagabonda" print evening gown made of Antron nylon and designed by Gene Berk for Paganne. The dress was sold at Hudson's, I.Magnin, Lord & Taylor and Sakowitz in 1974.

Cranberry and gold foil beads form a classy draped necklace. The color is repeated in the dangle earrings made with cranberry beads and metal rings.

"Kutari" print dinner dress and halter pajamas of the same print made of Nyesta Antron nylon and designed by Gene Berk for Paganne. *Harper's Bazaar,* 1974

Amulet style necklace made of gold-plated metal and plastic beads made to look like gemstones in the rough. Tri-colored chain link dangle earrings by unknown maker.

A mural in earth tones made of Antron nylon and Lycra designed by Gene Berk for Paganne. This two-piece outfit retailed for $125.00 in 1974. *Harper's Bazaar*, February, 1974

Another variation of Gene Berks' mural signature print, this time designed as a day dress and in a different color combination. *Harper's Bazaar*, February, 1974

In the use and extent of design sources, conversation prints rage widely and imaginatively, with antic delight, over subjects sophisticated and sportive, humorous and historical. Anything goes in conversation prints today.
American Fabrics, Fall-Winter, 1963

Close-up of the Paganne signature located at the bottom of the dress near the hemline. Surprisingly, this signature is not accompanied by the copyright symbol like most of the later prints.

An Erte on Antron nylon signed Paganne and labeled Paganne Ltd. by Gene Berk. This was an extremely popular print. It was also offered in different color schemes and styles of dress. Light blue peau de soie open toe sling-backs by Charles Jourdan, Paris.

Right:
A black and white Pop Art print strategically placed on bright red ribbed knit created a knockout dress with flower power. The dress is signed Paganne. Woven fabrics with texture were perfect canvases for textile designers since the print appeared to have more depth and added dimension when applied to a textured surface. Black patent leather pumps with glitter inserts by Imperial.

Opposite page:
Exceptional hand-manipulated draped neckpiece made of faux pearls, ruby red glass beads and faceted clear crystals by Mimi di N. The oversized jeweled earrings designed with a clever assortment of faux gemstones are unmarked.

Below:
Close-up of the Paganne signature with the copyright symbol.

Turquoise thermoplastic cabochons in fancy silvertone settings form a bracelet and matching clip earring set marked Coro. Triple-strand faceted turquoise plastic draped necklace marked West Germany. Jeweled canvas bag by Enid Collins and signed **ec** with the copyright symbol.

A solid black ribbed bodice compliments the abstract printed skirt with Empire waist and side slit signed Paganne. The two-toned gray high-heeled pumps are labeled Aj.Valenci, Made in Spain.

Chunky bead necklace composed of coral-colored Lucite beads in unusual shapes accented with goldtone spacer beads by unknown maker. Hinged bracelet of textured gold plate and coral cabochons designed by Pauline Rader. Ring made of large faux coral cabochon set in goldtone metal.

A calming color palette of coral, pink and lavender in combination with a mixture of geometrics and florals was the perfect recipe for a soothing silhouette signed ©Paganne. Gold leather peep toe sling backs by Andrea Pfister.

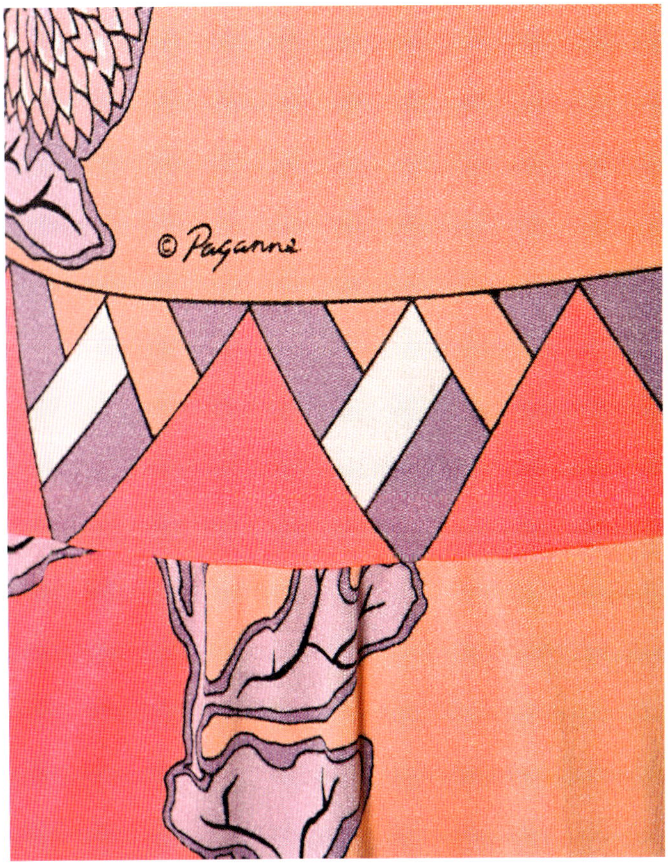

A closer view of the Paganne signature with the copyright symbol.

Grecian-style dress designed by Gene Berk for Paganne. This toga dress was made of silky Qiana and retailed for $125.00 in 1973. This dress was featured in the December issue of *Vogue* for that year.

Fashion excitement was generated with this clever *trompe-l'oeil* style print signed Paganne. A Lucite pendant enhanced with ornamental gold-plated metal is suspended from a Lucite bead chain. The oversized gold-plated filigree and clear Lucite earrings are unmarked. Tan and black leather t-straps by Gucci, Made in Italy.

Choker necklace and bracelet demi-parure of red and black Lucite encased in fancy silver-plated metal further accented with rhinestones, unknown maker.

The Greek influence on fabric and fashion design is growing. What is merely a ground-swell at the moment should develop into a full-fledged style trend within the next year or two.
American Fabrics, Summer, 1960

A bold color scheme coupled with a Greek-inspired print created the right amount of fashion drama in this long sleeve, v-necked shift signed Paganne. Black silk pumps with rhinestone buckles by Gianni.

It would be a mistake to regard the festive fringe as purely casual embellishment. A border of fringe, purposefully added to an otherwise prosaic item of apparel, has an innocently bold look about it that says "Stop and look!" while it gives a lighthearted air to the wearer.
American Fabrics, Summer, 1963

A sleeveless Empire gown of Antron nylon with a plunging neckline is further enhanced with a matching fringed shawl. Paganne signatures are found amidst the large blooms and the geometrics in this black and white silhouette from 1972. Lucite rosebuds, made to look like frosted glass were accented with French jet and rhinestones to create this stunning demi-parure by Diane von Furstenburg. Black suede ankle strap heels by Premiere Collection.

Black and white floral print dress with matching fringed shawl designed by Gene Berk for Paganne. *Vogue*, February, 1972

A fitted and jeweled bodice with a voluminous skirt coupled with a dynamic black and white asymmetrical print screams fashion drama by Paganne. These elegant open-toe heels made of silver metallic leather accented with pave' rhinestones are fit for a queen. The shoes are labeled RAVNE Ltd., Appointment to Her Majesty the Queen Shoemaker. The crystal and rhinestone pendant necklace is signed Miriam Haskell. The rhinestone bracelet is marked Ciner.

An Egyptian motif with black and white definition made of Antron nylon was designed by Gene Berk for Paganne. Black silk pumps with sexy straps and clear rhinestone buckles by Gianni.

A wide gunmetal-colored Lucite bangle bracelet with mother of pearl inserts was styled by Accessocraft. Flapper-style necklace made of black and white beads with long tassel is unmarked.

A close-up view of the ©Paganne signature preceded by the copyright symbol.

Two versions of Gene Berks' white engineered print on a solid black dress, made of textured Antron nylon in 1972. The long dress retailed for $78.00; the short dress was $52.00.

Mod necklace of black and white plastic disks assembled with a three-dimensional approach by an unknown maker. French jet and rhinestone clip earrings made to look like crowns by Albert Weiss. A close-up of the Paganne signature on the sleeve shows it in an upside-down position. The earlier prints had the signature but not the copyright symbol.

The almost instantaneous adoption of Op Art by the textile, fashion and home furnishings industries is a significant demonstration of the speed with which things move in today's fabric and fashion world.
American Fabrics, Summer, 1965

A sexy Ban Lon chemise with an Op Art print in black and white has its own self-tied belt and an added plastic link belt. The dress is signed Paganne.

ROBERTA DI CAMERINO

Close-up of the belted **R** signature. Hinged bracelet made of gold-plated metal with block initials.

A 1960s interpretation of a cleverly deceptive painting technique called *trompe-l'oeil* which Roberta di Camerino became famous for by hand printing all of the design details onto fabric. These innovative garments used graphics to create design. This one piece jersey knit shirtdress appears to be a three-piece suit. Also referred to as "historical panel dresses," these garments are signed with the famous signature which is a belted letter **R**. Two-toned gray pumps by Aj.Valenci, Spain. Teal and gold draped necklace, unmarked.

Jersey shirtdress with *trompe-l'oeil* design by Roberta di Camerino. Samba shoes in olive green leather by Di Ferrarezzi, Brazil.

When you hear the name Robert di Camerino, instinctively you think of the wonderful, handcrafted, Venetian style velvet handbags, as well as her exotic bags made in crocodile, python, shaved mink, and fine leathers that are extremely coveted by collectors and customers all over the world.

After World War II, and out of necessity, Giuliana Camerino, later known as Roberta di Camerino, began making handbags in Italy. After one of her handbags was spotted on a lovely Italian model by Stanley Marcus, president of the Neiman Marcus stores, he set out to meet the designer.

Using velvet from an old textiles mill in Venice, that supplied the Vatican with handloomed fabrics for upholstery and vestments, Giuliana made a handbag at Marcus's request for his wife using a piece of cloth that Marcus purchased at the mill. Slightly taken aback by the thought of making a handbag from upholstery fabric, Camerino created the bag for Marcus, and the rest is history. Her career took off in the mid-1950s, when she received the Neiman Marcus "Oscar of Fashion" Award.

Working with the textile weavers in Venice, her famous *trompe-l'oeil* ideas were born. This elusive designer became a master of the arts, using apparel as her canvas. By the early 1960s, Roberta di Camerino was famous not only for her gorgeous bags, but also for her totally creative and innovative historical panel dresses that are extremely sought-after today.

SERBIN

Zodiac print shirtdress with Baroque detailing signed Serbin. Handcrafted basket purse decorated with beads, stones and gold appliqués by Midas of Miami. Black strappy sandals add the finishing touch.

Right: Triangular-shaped citrine-colored rhinestones, accented with smaller topaz glass stones were set in gold-plated metal to create a stunning Art Deco style choker necklace by unknown maker. Hinged bracelet and matching earrings set with unusual faux gemstones are signed Sarah Coventry.

Closer view of the Serbin signature discreetly hidden in the print.

Choker necklace of unusual branch-shaped metal and dome-shaped Peking glass further accented with emerald green rhinestones. Drop earrings with opaque green glass stones signed Bellini; mod ring and plastic bangle, unmarked. The Serbin signature is found on the cuff.

A bouquet of flowers on a cotton jersey shirt dress takes shape with a self-tied belt. The dress is signed and labeled Serbin. Other information gathered from the label also states that the dress was designed by Marianne. Many other signed Serbin dresses were labeled Serbin of Florida and designed by Muriel Ryan. Multi-colored suede slip-on wedgies stamped Made in Italy.

ALFRED SHAHEEN

Hand-screened over-sized tulip print dress with solid green fitted bodice and polyester skirt accented with a long green looped sash. The dress is signed Shaheen near the hemline. Royal blue peep toe pumps by Claudio Rocco.

Oversized Egyptian-styled neckpiece with a simulated lapis lazuli scarab and faux lapis and turquoise beads and stones. Similarly designed dangle earrings, makers unknown.

The POWer of the flower continues to amaze us. Prints bloom, grow bigger; see an oversized super spring on the avenues! Bigness does not mean lack of restraint; there is as much good taste in grandiose designs as there is in Lilliputia.
American Fabrics, Summer, 1968

The panel print you might say, is most probably and logically an inevitable development of the border prints which have been widely used for the past few years. With the almost insatiable demand for shifts, it was to be expected that the need would arise for print patterns that corresponded to the structure of the shift itself.
American Fabrics, Summer, 1963

Oversized hand-screened exotic blooms cascade down the front as well as the back of this maxi dress signed Shaheen. The solid bodice in royal blue is a nice compliment to the overall silhouette. A long looped sash adds the finishing touches.

Royal blue bib necklace with matching cluster earrings by unknown maker. An enameled and jeweled hinged serpent bracelet was designed by Panetta. Costume ring of blue glass and filigree metal, unmarked.

Alfred Shaheen was in business for 40 years creating spectacular aloha fashions for men and women. What makes Shaheen unique to Hawaii was the fact that he designed the prints on the fabrics in addition to designing the apparel. After serving his time in World War II, Shaheen returned home to Hawaii and began working in the family garment business. Wanting to expand what his parents had already started, Shaheen realized that creating custom fabrics instead of having them imported from the mainland was the smart thing to do. He set out to build his own machinery and opened his first print plant in a Quonset hut. He named the business Surf n' Sand Hand Prints. He employed four seamstresses that learned the trade from Shaheen's mother. His business flourished and by 1956, he was able to build a multi-million dollar manufacturing company. By 1960, he had over 400 employees. He opened a chain of retail stores all across the Hawaiian Islands. Shaheen was the largest manufacturer of aloha wear in Hawaii during the fifties and sixties. Sarongs, swim suits, cover-ups, sundresses, evening dresses and Hawaiian shirts were mass-produced with his unique style.

Close-up of Shaheen signature found in the print done in gold script. Royal blue pumps by Claudio Rocco.

A textured polyester panel print of exotic flora and fauna is rendered in shades of coral, melon, green and gold. The maxi dress has sheer sleeves and a self-tied belt. The dress is signed Shaheen.

A demi-parure of melon-colored thermoset plastic set in goldtone metal. Expansion bracelet made of elongated segments of coral-colored plastic, unknown makers.

Close-up of the Shaheen signature in gold script found at the bottom of the dress near the hemline. Gold metallic leather criss-cross mules designed by Peppers, Italy.

Shaheen's inspiration was drawn from his homeland as well as travels to the South Pacific and Asia. He loved exotic flora and fauna, which he creatively used again and again. The Shaheen signature can be found on many of his prints. Shaheen had numerous labels on his different lines of clothing and he also manufactured clothing for other retailers as well. He believed in being true to his culture and ethnic background and his handprints were a reflection of his beliefs. Today, many of his exotic sarong dresses, bathing suits and aloha shirts are commanding high prices. Signed clothing by Alfred Shaheen is extremely desirable.

Alfred Shaheen created black and white fashion excitement when he designed this day dress with hand-screened and fitted bodice and full pleated skirt. Black patent leather pumps with lacy suede straps by Rush Hour Express.

Hand painted bangle bracelet with black and white geometric patterns. White plastic drop earrings made in the mod style of the 1960s. The black and white plastic disk necklace is unmarked.

Close-up of the Shaheen signature found on the hand-screened bodice near the waistline.

Asian-inspired polyester gown with plunging neckline, Empire waist, wide sash and hand-screened print signed Shaheen. Four-strand bib neckpiece made of French jet, clear crystal beads and fluted gold-plated beads by Napier.

Close-up of the Shaheen signature near the hemline. The signature on many of Alfred Shaheen's prints is found at this location on the garment. Fabric and leather pumps designed by Kenneth Cole, New York.

Close-up of the Shaheen signature in gold script. The turquoise leather mules with extraordinary leather floral decoration were designed by Bonnie Smith for Kimel.

Lovely nylon and polyester hand-screened panel prints with an Asian motif rendered in shades of turquoise and lavender. The dress has sheer sleeves, buttons down the front and is signed Shaheen. The Alfred Shaheen hang tags still accompany this dress and specific care instructions were given. These dresses were to be hand washed in pure soap in warm water. It went on to say that Woolite was cold water soap and was not to be used as it could damage the Shaheen handprints. Oversized three-dimensional ruffled brooch set with faux amethyst keystones in rhodium-plated metal signed Schreiner. Bracelet and earring set of gold-plated metal and amethyst glass stones, unmarked.

We like the black and white prints, the Indians, the gypsies, the swirls, the girls, the flag, the stars and stripes; in fact, nearly everything that has become a print. The field is wide open.
American Fabrics, Spring, 1969

Two-piece polyester outfit with hand-screened patriotic print signed Shaheen. The solid white top and red, white and blue maxi skirt unite with the bright red sash. The polka dot bangle bracelet of multi-colored Lucite was styled by Accessocraft.

Japanese glass made to look Venetian coupled with plastic creates a necklace with a red, white and blue theme. Blue and white mod earrings made of plastic marked West Germany.

Close-up of Shaheen signature found above the stars near the hemline.

TRISSI

Close-up of the trissi signature accompanied by the copyright symbol.

Sleeveless button-down polyester blouse made in the mod style of the 1960s with circular designs rendered in psychedelic colors. The blouse is signed ©trissi and it was manufactured by trissi, Inc., a New York based manufacturing company of women's sportswear. Genuine DuPont Lucite bangle bracelets in pink and green; mod shoulder duster two-toned plastic earrings made in West Germany; chevron designed lattice-style necklace enameled in bright green, unmarked.

Heavy weight polyester button-down blouse with a dynamic Op Art print signed ©trissi. Silvertone metal with shiny mirrored surfaces was designed by Bill de Seta for Accessocraft.

Close-up of the ©trissi signature accompanied by the copyright symbol.

Close-up of the ©trissi signature, again accompanied by the copyright symbol.

In 1958, bold patterned silk shirts by the designer Pucci set a trend in the Riviera, Florida and Caribbean resort areas. The effect of this brilliant Pucci styling is now beginning to broaden out into an exciting group of conversation-piece prints which will soon move into the volume field. We believe it is a logical contender for the next big direction in prints.
American Fabrics, Fall-Winter, 1960

Button-down blouse of heavy polyester with an Asian-inspired panel print. The blouse is signed ©trissi. Basket handbag with plastic fruit and flower decoration by unknown maker; jeweled choker necklace by Schauer, Fifth Avenue, New York.

VERA

Known for her "sumi brushwork" techniques like Japanese painters, Vera Neumann, the American print and textile designer created this silk blouse with large blooms in her style that she became famous for. It was more of an abstract form that was described as being *always un-stereotyped, deceptively simple, and very sophisticated,* according to **American Fabrics**. Fine detail was secondary to creating the essence of the actual object.

A large Vera signature without the ladybug and copyright symbol date this blouse to the mid-to-late sixties. Demi-parure designed with a large pendant necklace made of concentric circles of clear and faux emerald rhinestones with matching drop earrings by Schreiner. A glitzy wide emerald green and clear rhinestone bracelet has no identifying marks.

A Ban Lon mini-dress was printed with blocks of neon colors coupled with black and white abstract prints. The dress was designed with a stand-up collar and self-tied belt. Dating back to the mid-to-late sixties, this dress is signed Vera. The mod earrings were made of two-toned pink plastic, unmarked. The long ball and chain necklace was made with speckled composition beads and japanned metal chain. The black skin tight boots add more fashion drama.

The company created by Vera and George Neumann and F. Werner Hamm in 1946 became an American success story. Encouraged by her husband who was the head of a screen printing plant called Printex in Ossining, New York, Vera as able to create the designs which the plant was able to mass produce. Uniting the love for hand crafted work with the technology of mass production, Vera textiles became an international sensation for many decades. Vera scarves were sold just about everywhere after World War II, even in many of the European countries and Australia.

As popularity increased, blouses, dresses, ascots and even table linens, towels and drapery fabrics were designed by Vera. Sometimes a single theme would be reproduced on many different products. The simplest form, such as a strawberry or a fern would be the basis for the entire line. The sophisticated hostess of the sixties would set her table in Vera linens and wear a matching apron. Vera's signature appeared on everything. Throughout the fifties and up until the mid-to-late sixties, her signature ladybug stood beside her name. Around 1968, the copyright symbol appeared. Shortly after, the ladybug disappeared. Throughout the sixties Vera ads were found in women's magazines of the day. Her unique style was loved by all.

Wide legged pants and printed tunic top made of cotton and signed Vera. *Vogue*, December, 1968

In the mid-to-late sixties, the Vera signature became slightly larger. The ladybug was also removed as well as the copyright symbol.

Boldness and bravado describe this polished cotton blouse in red, white and blue signed Vera©.

The ladybug is Vera's signature. When a Vera ad in "Seventeen" offered a ladybug pin to anyone sending in the name of their favorite Vera store, the firm was overwhelmed by 27,000 letters.
American Fabrics, Winter-Spring, 1964

Multi-strand beaded necklace made of tiny red, white and blue beads. Mod earrings made of thin plastic strips in red and white were designed by Paco Rabanne. Wide link bracelet in bright red enamel is unmarked.

Close-up of the Vera© signature with the copyright symbol dating this blouse to the early seventies.

SIGNATURE SCARVES

Here's a thought. If you love signature prints, why not start a collection of signature print scarves. The choices are endless and you can still find many at reasonable prices. Here we have a very small sampling of what is available to collectors. Emilio Pucci, Leo Narducci, Elsa Schiaparelli, Rudi Gernreich and Vera scarves are pictured.

It may not be new to the models that flit about on New York's avenues and side streets, but the whole vogue for head scarves is still in its infancy. The fashion becomes more and more widespread with recognition of its decorativeness and practical-ness at such a small cost.
American Fabrics, Fall, 1964

BIBLIOGRAPHY

Books

Bender, Marilyn. *The Beautiful People.* New York: Coward-McCann, Inc., 1967.

Carter, Ernestine. *Magic Names of Fashion.* Englewood Cliffs, New Jersey: Prentice-Hall Inc., 1980.

Casadio, Mariuccia. *Emilio Pucci.* New York: The Universe Press, 1998.

Ettinger, Roseann. *20th Century Plastic Jewelry.* Atglen, Pennsylvania: Schiffer Publishing Ltd., 2007.

Ettinger, Roseann. *Popular Jewelry of the 60s, 70s & 80s.* Atglen, Pennsylvania: Schiffer Publishing Ltd., 1997.

Ettinger, Roseann. *Psychedelic Chic: Artistic Fashions of the Late 1960s and Early 1970s.* Atglen, Pennsylvania: Schiffer Publishing Ltd., 1999.

Kennedy, Shirley. *Pucci: A Renaissance in Fashion.* New York: Abbeville Press, 1991.

Marcus, Stanley. *Minding the Store.* Canada: Little, Brown & Company Limited, 1974.

Marcus, Stanley. *Quest for the Best.* New York: The Viking Press, 1979.

Periodicals

American Fabrics, Issues 34 to 80; 1955 to 1969.

Domenica del Corriere, 1971.

Glamour, January, 1955.

Harper's Bazaar, July, 1961, August and November, 1964, December, 1967, October, 1969, March to November, 1971, November and December, 1973, May, 1974 and April, 1976, June, 2006.

Ladies' Home Journal, July and August, 1963, December, 1966.

Life, August 21, 1970.

McCall's, December, 1966.

Time, October, 1969.

Vogue, May to October, 1964, June to December, 1966, December, 1967, September and December, 1968, February, 1969, April, 1970, January, 1971, January to December, 1972, September, 1973, and February, 1974.

Newspapers

The Palladium Times, December 20, 1967

Websites

hrrp://www.answers.com

http://www.braniffinternational.org

http://www.chelseamarketeers.com/BraniffGeminiIV3.htm

http://www.fashionunited.co.uk/news/pucci.htm

http://www.lillypulitzer.com

http://www.mildredhoit.com/abessi.html

http://www.musee-des-tissus.com: Daniel Tribouillard, History of Leonard.

http://www.robertadicamerino.com

http://www.vintagefashionguild.org

INDEX